WORLD SILVER COIN VALUE GUIDE

BY
LORRAINE S. DURST
&
SANFORD J. DURST

Sanford J. Durst
Numismatic Publications
New York, N.Y.

133 East 58th Street
New York, N.Y. 10022

ISBN No 0-915262-46-0

Library Congress No. 80-51831

The information contained herein is from sources deemed reliable. No guarantee express or implied is made with regard to the accuracy of information in this book, and the publisher for itself its employees, agents, or distributors hereby disclaims any liability with regard to the use of the data presented herein.

TABLE OF CONTENTS

INTRODUCTION

The need for an easy-to-use valuation book for world silver coinage has never been more important than at the present time.

With silver now fluctuating in the $30.00-$50.00 price range and world political affairs and monetary uncertainties possibly pushing the values of the metal and coins made of silver higher, the bullion value of a coin has in many instances surpassed its numismatic worth, temporarily, if not permanently.

Meltage of these items threatens to put a big dent in the availability of numismatic items in future years.

Accordingly, it is of great value to numismatists, investors, dealers, bullion purchasers and sellers to instantly know the worth of a coin. For their assistance, we have prepared, in easy to use, concise form, this value guide.

Coins are included by types. Older coins, for which it is only remotely possible that they will be deemed bullion, have been omitted. So called NCLT (Non-circulating legal tender) are included because they are held in quantity and have been offered on the market on a bullion or near bullion basis for some time. Proofs generally have the same metal content as coins produced for circulation and only where there is a variance, are they included. Conversion tables are included on important weights and measures.

This guide is easily usable by those familiar with foreign currencies such as SFr, £, D.M., etc., by simple multiplication, once the U.S. dollar value, appearing in our tabulations, is obtained.

We are aware that these statistics are available in scattered form in coin sales brochures, catalogs, etc., but are certain that the size, presentation and scope of this book will make it a most useful tool.

Lorraine S. Durst
Sanford J. Durst

WEIGHTS AND MEASURES

Purity:

24 carats	=	1000 fine (pure gold)
22 carats	=	916⅔ fine
21 19/32 carats	=	900 fine
21 carats	=	875 fine
18 carats	=	750 fine
14 carats	=	583⅓ fine
1 carat	=	41.67 fine

Weights:

1 Troy oz.	=	31.103 grams
1 Troy oz.	=	480 grains
32.15 oz.	=	1000 grams (1 kilogram)
1 grain	=	0.0648 grams
1 gram	=	0.643 pennyweight
1000 grams	=	1 kilogram
1 Troy oz.	=	20 pennyweight
1 Avoirdupois oz.	=	28.34 grams
1 Avoirdupois oz.	=	.911 Troy oz.
35.274 Avoirdupois oz.	=	1 kilogram

Sizes:

Inches	Millimeters
1/4	6.35
1/2	12.70
3/4	19.05
1	25.40
1¼	31.75
1½	38.10
1¾	44.45
2	50.08

Coin Denomination	Years of Issue	Coin Wt. Grams	Purity	Silver Wt. Grams	Silver Troy Oz.	Silver Value—U.S. Dollars $1	$2	$4	$6	$8	$10	$20	$30	$40	$50	$60	$70	$80	$90	$100
AFGHANISTAN																				
1/2 RUPEE	1919-1924	5.00	916	4.58	0.15	.15	.30	.60	.90	1.20	1.50	3.00	4.50	6.00	7.50	9.00	10.50	12.00	13.50	15.00
1 RUPEE	1901-1930	10.00	916	9.16	0.29	.29	.58	1.16	1.74	2.32	2.90	5.80	8.70	11.60	14.50	17.40	18.90	23.20	26.10	29.00
2-1/2 RUPEE	1919-1924	25.00	916	22.90	0.74	.74	1.48	2.96	4.44	5.92	7.40	14.80	22.20	29.60	37.00	44.40	51.80	59.20	66.60	74.00
5 RUPEE	1901-1919	45.00	916	41.22	1.33	1.33	2.66	5.32	7.98	10.64	13.30	26.60	39.90	53.20	66.50	79.80	93.10	106.40	119.70	133.00
1/2 AFGHANI	1926-1937	5.00	916	4.58	0.15	.15	.30	.60	.90	1.20	1.50	3.00	4.50	6.00	7.50	9.00	10.50	12.00	13.50	15.00
1 AFGHANI	1926-1928	10.00	916	9.16	0.29	.29	.58	1.16	1.74	2.32	2.90	5.80	8.70	11.60	14.50	17.40	18.90	23.20	26.10	29.00
2-1/2 AFGHANI	1927-1928	25.00	916	22.90	0.74	.74	1.48	2.96	4.44	5.92	7.40	14.80	22.20	29.60	37.00	44.40	51.80	59.20	66.60	74.00
250 AFGHANI	1978	28.30	925	26.16	0.84	.84	1.68	3.36	5.04	6.72	8.40	16.80	25.20	33.60	42.00	50.40	58.80	67.20	75.60	84.00
500 AFGHANI	1978	35.00	925	32.17	1.03	1.03	2.06	4.12	6.18	8.24	10.30	20.60	30.90	41.20	51.50	61.80	72.10	82.40	92.70	103.00
AJMAN																				
1 RIYAL	1969-1970	3.90	640	2.49	0.08	.08	.16	.32	.48	.64	.80	1.60	2.40	3.20	4.00	4.80	5.60	6.40	7.20	8.00
2 RIYALS	1969-1970	6.50	835	5.42	0.17	.17	.34	.68	1.02	1.36	1.70	3.40	5.10	6.80	8.50	10.20	11.90	13.60	15.30	17.00
5 RIYALS	1969	15.00	835	12.52	0.40	.40	.80	1.60	2.40	3.20	4.00	8.00	12.00	16.00	20.00	24.00	28.00	32.00	36.00	40.00
5 RIYALS	1970-1971	15.10	835	12.60	0.41	.41	.82	1.64	2.46	3.28	4.10	8.20	12.30	16.40	20.50	24.60	28.70	32.80	36.90	41.00
7-1/2 RIYALS	1970	23.00	925	21.30	0.68	.68	1.36	2.72	4.08	5.44	6.80	13.60	20.40	27.20	34.00	40.80	47.60	54.40	61.20	68.00
7-1/2 RIYALS	NASSAR1970	23.00	835	19.20	0.62	.62	1.24	2.48	3.72	4.96	6.20	12.40	18.60	24.80	31.00	37.20	43.40	49.60	55.80	62.00
10 RIYALS	1970	29.90	925	27.70	0.89	.89	1.78	3.56	5.34	7.12	8.90	17.80	26.70	35.60	44.50	53.40	62.30	71.20	80.10	89.00
ALBANIA																				
1 FRANGA-AVI	1927-1937	5.00	835	4.17	0.13	.13	.26	.52	.78	1.04	1.30	2.60	3.90	5.20	6.50	7.80	9.10	10.40	11.70	13.00
2 FRANGA-AVI	1926-1937	10.00	900	9.00	0.29	.29	.58	1.16	1.74	2.32	2.90	5.80	8.70	11.60	14.50	17.40	18.90	23.20	26.10	29.00
5 FRANGA-AVI	1926	25.00	900	22.50	0.72	.72	1.44	2.88	4.32	5.76	7.20	14.40	21.60	28.80	37.00	43.20	50.40	57.60	64.80	72.00
5 LEK	1939	5.00	835	4.17	0.13	.13	.26	.52	.78	1.04	1.30	2.60	3.90	5.20	6.50	7.80	9.10	10.40	11.70	13.00
10 LEK	1939	10.00	1000	10.00	0.32	.32	.64	1.28	1.92	2.56	3.20	6.40	9.60	12.80	16.00	19.20	22.40	25.60	28.80	32.00
5 LEKE	1968-1970	16.16	1000	16.16	0.52	.52	1.04	2.08	3.12	4.16	5.20	10.40	15.60	20.80	26.00	31.20	36.40	41.60	46.80	52.00
10 LEKE	1968-1970	33.33	1000	33.33	1.07	1.07	2.14	4.28	6.42	8.56	10.70	21.40	32.10	42.80	53.50	64.20	74.90	85.60	96.30	107.00
25 LEKE	1968-1970	83.33	1000	83.33	2.68	2.68	5.36	10.72	16.08	21.44	26.80	53.60	80.40	107.00	134.00	160.80	187.60	214.40	241.20	268.00
ALGERIA																				
5 DINARS	1972	12.00	750	9.00	0.29	.29	.58	1.16	1.74	2.32	2.90	5.80	8.70	11.60	14.50	17.40	18.90	23.20	26.10	29.00
ANDORRA																				
25 DINERS	1963-1965	31.70	990	13.60	0.44	.44	.88	1.76	2.64	3.52	4.40	8.80	13.20	17.60	22.00	26.40	30.80	35.20	39.60	44.00
50 DINERS	1963-1965	28.00	990	27.70	0.89	.89	1.78	3.56	5.34	7.12	8.90	17.80	26.70	35.60	44.50	53.40	62.30	71.20	80.10	89.00

Coin Denomination	Years of Issue	Coin Wt. Grams	Purity	Silver Wt. Grams	Silver Troy Oz.	Silver Value—U.S. Dollars														
						$1	$2	$4	$6	$8	$10	$20	$30	$40	$50	$60	$70	$80	$90	$100
ANGOLA																				
10 ESCUDOS	1952-1955	5.00	720	3.60	0.12	.12	.24	.48	.72	.96	1.20	2.40	3.60	4.80	6.00	7.20	8.40	9.60	10.80	12.00
20 ESCUDOS	1952-1955	10.00	720	7.20	0.23	.23	.46	.92	1.38	1.84	2.30	4.60	6.90	9.20	11.50	13.80	16.10	18.40	20.70	23.00
ANGUILLA																				
1/2 DOLLAR	1967-1970	3.57	1000	3.57	0.11	.11	.22	.44	.66	.88	1.10	2.20	3.30	4.40	5.50	6.60	7.70	8.80	9.90	11.00
1 DOLLAR	1967-1970	7.14	1000	7.14	0.23	.23	.46	.92	1.38	1.84	2.30	4.60	6.90	9.20	11.50	13.80	16.10	18.40	20.70	23.00
2 DOLLARS	1967-1970	14.30	1000	14.30	0.46	.46	.92	1.84	2.76	3.68	4.60	9.20	13.80	18.40	23.00	27.60	32.20	36.80	41.40	46.00
4 DOLLARS	1967-1970	28.60	1000	28.60	0.92	.92	1.84	3.68	5.52	7.36	9.20	18.40	27.60	36.80	46.00	55.20	64.40	73.60	82.80	92.00
25 DOLLARS	1974	31.00	999	31.00	1.00	1.00	2.00	4.00	6.00	8.00	10.00	20.00	30.00	40.00	50.00	60.00	70.00	80.00	90.00	100.00
ARGENTINA																				
10CENTAVOS	1881-1883	2.50	900	2.25	0.07	.07	.14	.28	.42	.56	.70	1.40	2.10	2.80	3.50	4.20	4.90	5.60	6.30	7.00
20CENTAVOS	1881-1883	5.00	900	4.50	0.14	.14	.28	.56	.84	1.12	1.40	2.80	4.20	5.60	7.00	8.40	9.80	11.20	12.60	14.00
50CENTAVOS	1881-1883	12.50	900	11.25	0.36	.36	.72	1.44	2.16	2.88	3.60	7.20	10.80	14.40	18.00	21.60	25.20	28.80	32.40	36.00
1 PESO	1881-1883	25.00	900	22.50	0.72	.72	1.44	2.88	4.32	5.76	7.20	14.40	21.60	28.80	36.00	43.20	50.40	57.60	64.80	72.00
1000 PESOS	1977-1978	10.00	900	9.00	0.29	.29	.58	1.16	1.74	2.32	2.90	5.80	8.70	11.60	14.50	17.40	18.90	23.20	26.10	29.00
2000 PESOS	1977-1978	15.00	900	13.50	0.43	.43	.86	1.72	2.58	3.44	4.30	8.60	12.90	17.20	21.50	25.80	30.10	34.40	38.70	43.00
3000 PESOS	1977-1978	25.00	900	22.50	0.70	.70	1.40	2.80	4.20	5.60	7.00	14.00	21.00	28.00	35.00	42.00	49.00	56.00	63.00	70.00
ASCENSION ISLAND																				
1 CROWN	1978	28.30	925	26.20	0.84	.84	1.68	3.36	5.04	6.72	8.40	16.80	25.20	33.60	42.00	50.40	58.80	67.20	75.60	84.00
AUSTRALIA																				
3 PENCE	1910-1944	1.40	925	1.30	0.04	.04	.08	.16	.24	.32	.40	.80	1.20	1.60	2.00	2.40	2.80	3.20	3.60	4.00
3 PENCE	1947-1964	1.40	500	0.70	0.03	.03	.06	.12	.18	.24	.30	.60	.90	1.20	1.50	1.80	2.10	2.40	2.70	3.00
6 PENCE	1910-1945	2.80	925	2.60	0.08	.08	.16	.32	.48	.64	.80	1.60	2.40	3.20	4.00	4.80	5.60	6.40	7.20	8.00
6 PENCE	1946-1963	2.80	500	1.40	0.05	.05	.10	.20	.30	.40	.50	1.00	1.50	2.00	2.50	3.00	3.50	4.00	4.50	5.00
1 SHILLING	1910-1945	5.66	925	5.30	0.17	.17	.34	.68	1.02	1.36	1.70	3.40	5.10	6.80	8.50	10.20	11.90	13.60	15.30	17.00
1 SHILLING	1946-1963	5.66	500	2.80	0.09	.09	.18	.36	.54	.72	.90	1.80	2.70	3.60	4.50	5.40	6.30	7.20	8.10	9.00
1 FLORIN	1910-1944	11.30	925	10.50	0.38	.38	.76	1.52	2.28	3.04	3.80	7.60	11.40	15.20	19.00	22.80	26.60	30.40	34.20	38.00
1 FLORIN	1946-1963	11.30	500	5.60	0.18	.18	.36	.72	1.08	1.44	1.80	3.60	5.40	7.20	9.00	10.80	12.60	14.40	16.20	18.00
1 CROWN	1937-1938	28.30	925	26.20	0.84	.84	1.68	3.36	5.04	6.72	8.40	16.80	25.20	33.60	42.00	50.40	58.80	67.20	75.60	84.00
50 CENTS	1966	13.30	800	10.60	0.34	.34	.68	1.36	2.04	2.72	3.40	6.80	10.20	13.60	17.00	20.40	23.80	27.20	30.60	34.00

Coin Denomination	Years of Issue	Coin Wt. Grams	Purity	Silver Wt. Grams	Silver Troy Oz.	Silver Value—U.S. Dollars $1	$2	$4	$6	$8	$10	$20	$30	$40	$50	$60	$70	$80	$90	$100
AUSTRIA																				
1 FLORIN	1857-1892	12.34	900	11.10	0.36	.36	.72	1.44	2.16	2.88	3.60	7.20	10.80	14.40	18.00	21.60	25.20	28.80	32.40	36.00
2 FLORIN	1859-1892	24.70	900	22.20	0.71	.71	1.42	2.84	4.26	5.68	7.10	14.20	21.30	28.40	35.50	42.60	49.70	56.80	63.90	71.00
1 VERREIN- STALER	1857-1867	18.50	900	16.60	0.53	.53	1.06	2.12	3.18	4.24	5.30	10.60	15.90	21.20	26.50	31.80	37.10	42.40	47.70	53.00
1 KRONE	1892-1916	5.00	835	4.20	0.14	.14	.28	.56	.84	1.12	1.40	2.80	4.20	5.60	7.00	8.40	9.80	11.20	12.60	14.00
2 KRONEN	1912-1913	10.00	835	8.40	0.27	.27	.54	1.08	1.62	2.16	2.70	5.40	8.10	10.80	13.50	16.20	18.90	21.60	24.30	27.00
5 KRONEN	1900-1909	24.00	900	21.60	0.69	.69	1.38	2.76	4.14	5.52	6.90	13.80	20.70	27.60	34.50	41.40	48.30	55.20	62.10	69.00
1/2 SCHILLING	1925-1926	3.00	640	1.90	0.06	.06	.12	.24	.36	.48	.60	1.20	1.80	2.40	3.00	3.60	4.20	4.80	5.40	6.00
1 SCHILLING	1925-1926	6.00	640	3.80	0.12	.12	.24	.48	.72	.96	1.20	2.40	3.60	4.80	6.00	7.20	8.40	9.60	10.80	12.00
1 SCHILLING	1924	7.00	800	5.60	0.18	.18	.36	.72	1.08	1.44	1.80	3.60	5.40	7.20	9.00	10.80	12.60	14.40	16.20	18.00
2 SCHILLING	1928-1937	12.00	640	7.70	0.25	.25	.50	1.00	1.50	2.00	2.50	5.00	7.50	10.00	12.50	15.00	17.50	20.00	22.50	25.00
5 SCHILLING	1934-1936	15.00	835	12.50	0.40	.40	.80	1.60	2.40	3.20	4.00	8.00	12.00	16.00	20.00	24.00	28.00	32.00	36.00	40.00
5 SCHILLING	1960-1968	5.20	640	3.30	0.11	.11	.22	.44	.66	.88	1.10	2.20	3.30	4.40	5.50	6.60	7.70	8.80	9.90	11.00
10SCHILLING	1957-1973	7.50	640	4.80	0.15	.15	.30	.60	.90	1.20	1.50	3.00	4.50	6.00	7.50	9.00	10.50	12.00	13.50	15.00
25SCHILLING	1957-1973	13.00	800	10.40	0.33	.33	.66	1.32	1.98	2.64	3.30	6.60	9.90	13.20	16.50	19.80	23.10	26.40	29.70	33.00
50SCHILLING	1959-1973	20.00	900	18.00	0.58	.58	1.16	2.32	3.48	4.64	5.80	11.60	17.40	23.20	29.00	34.80	40.60	46.40	52.20	58.00
50SCHILLING	1974	20.00	640	12.80	0.41	.41	.82	1.64	2.46	3.28	4.10	8.20	12.30	16.40	20.50	24.60	28.70	32.80	36.90	41.00
100 SCHILLING	1974-1980	24.00	640	15.40	0.50	.50	1.00	2.00	3.00	4.00	5.00	10.00	15.00	20.00	25.00	30.00	35.00	40.00	45.00	50.00
1 TALER	1780R	28.00	833	23.40	0.75	.75	1.50	3.00	4.50	6.00	7.50	15.00	22.50	30.00	37.50	45.00	52.50	60.00	67.50	75.00
BAHAMAS																				
50 CENTS	1966-1978	10.40	800	8.30	0.27	.27	.54	1.08	1.62	2.16	2.70	5.40	8.10	10.80	13.50	16.20	18.90	21.60	24.30	27.00
1 DOLLAR	1966-1978	18.10	800	14.50	0.47	.47	.94	1.88	2.82	3.76	4.70	9.40	14.10	18.80	23.50	28.20	32.90	37.60	42.30	47.00
2 DOLLARS	1966-1978	29.80	925	27.60	0.89	.89	1.78	3.56	5.34	7.12	8.90	17.80	26.70	35.60	44.50	53.40	62.30	71.20	80.10	89.00
5 DOLLARS	1966-1978	42.10	925	39.00	1.25	1.25	2.50	5.00	7.50	10.00	12.50	25.00	37.50	50.00	62.50	75.00	87.50	100.00	112.50	125.00
10 DOLLARS	1973-1977	48.60	925	45.00	1.45	1.45	2.90	5.80	8.70	11.60	14.50	29.00	43.50	58.00	72.50	87.00	101.50	116.00	130.50	145.00
10 DOLLARS	1978	45.40	500	22.70	0.73	.73	1.46	2.92	4.38	5.84	7.30	14.60	21.90	29.20	36.50	43.80	51.10	58.40	65.70	73.00
BAHRAIN																				
500 FILS	1968	18.30	800	14.60	0.47	.47	.94	1.88	2.82	3.76	4.70	9.40	14.10	18.80	23.50	28.20	32.90	37.60	42.30	47.00
BARBADOS																				
5 DOLLARS	1973-1976	29.50	800	23.60	0.76	.76	1.52	3.04	4.56	6.08	7.60	15.20	22.80	30.40	38.00	45.60	53.20	60.80	68.40	76.00
10 DOLLARS	1973-1976	35.50	925	32.90	1.06	1.06	2.12	4.24	6.36	8.48	10.60	21.20	31.80	42.40	53.00	63.60	74.20	84.80	95.40	106.00
25 DOLLARS	1978	27.30	925	25.20	0.81	.81	1.62	3.24	4.86	6.48	8.10	16.20	24.30	32.40	40.50	48.60	56.70	64.80	72.90	81.00

Coin Denomination	Years of Issue	Coin Wt. Grams	Purity	Silver Wt. Grams	Silver Troy Oz.	Silver Value—U.S. Dollars														
						$1	$2	$4	$6	$8	$10	$20	$30	$40	$50	$60	$70	$80	$90	$100
BELGIUM																				
50 CENTIMES	1866-1914	2.50	835	2.10	0.07	.07	.14	.28	.42	.56	.70	1.40	2.10	2.80	3.50	4.20	4.90	5.60	6.30	7.00
1 FRANC	1866-1914	5.00	835	4.20	0.14	.14	.28	.56	.84	1.12	1.40	2.80	4.20	5.60	7.00	8.40	9.80	11.20	12.60	14.00
2 FRANCS	1866-1912	10.00	835	8.40	0.27	.27	.54	1.08	1.62	2.16	2.70	5.40	8.10	10.80	13.50	16.20	18.90	21.60	24.30	27.00
5 FRANCS	1865-1876	25.00	900	22.50	0.72	.72	1.44	2.88	4.32	5.76	7.20	14.40	21.60	28.80	36.00	43.20	50.40	57.60	64.80	72.00
20 FRANCS	1933-1935	11.00	680	7.50	0.24	.24	.48	.96	1.44	1.92	2.40	4.80	7.20	9.60	12.00	14.40	16.80	19.20	21.60	24.00
20 FRANCS	1949-1955	8.00	835	6.70	0.22	.22	.44	.88	1.32	1.76	2.20	4.40	6.60	8.80	11.00	13.20	15.40	17.60	19.80	22.00
50 FRANCS	1939-1940	19.80	835	16.50	0.53	.53	1.06	2.12	3.18	4.24	5.30	10.60	15.90	21.20	26.50	31.80	37.10	42.40	47.70	53.00
50 FRANCS	1948-1960	12.50	835	10.40	0.33	.33	.66	1.32	1.98	2.64	3.30	6.60	9.90	13.20	16.50	19.80	23.10	26.40	29.70	33.00
100 FRANCS	1948-1951	18.00	835	15.00	0.48	.48	.96	1.92	2.88	3.84	4.80	9.60	14.40	19.20	24.00	28.80	33.60	38.40	43.20	48.00
250 FRANCS	1976	25.20	835	21.00	0.68	.68	1.36	2.72	4.08	5.44	6.80	13.60	20.40	27.20	34.00	40.80	47.60	54.40	61.20	68.00
BELIZE {BRITISH HONDURAS}																				
10 CENTS	1894-1946	2.30	925	2.10	0.07	.07	.14	.28	.42	.56	.70	1.40	2.10	2.80	3.50	4.20	4.90	5.60	6.30	7.00
25 CENTS	1894-1919	5.80	925	5.40	0.17	.17	.34	.68	1.02	1.36	1.70	3.40	5.10	6.80	8.50	10.20	11.90	13.60	15.30	17.00
50 CENTS	1894-1919	11.60	925	10.70	0.34	.34	.68	1.36	2.04	2.72	3.40	6.80	10.20	13.60	17.00	20.40	23.80	27.20	30.60	34.00
1 CENT	1974-1978	3.30	925	3.00	0.10	.10	.20	.40	.60	.80	1.00	2.00	3.00	4.00	5.00	6.00	7.00	8.00	9.00	10.00
5 CENTS	1974-1978	4.40	925	4.00	0.13	.13	.26	.52	.78	1.04	1.30	2.60	3.90	5.20	6.50	7.80	9.10	10.40	11.70	13.00
10 CENTS	1974-1978	2.70	925	2.50	0.80	.80	1.60	3.20	4.80	6.40	8.00	16.00	24.00	32.00	40.00	48.00	56.00	64.00	72.00	80.00
25 CENTS	1974-1978	6.50	925	6.00	0.19	.19	.38	.76	1.14	1.52	1.90	3.80	5.70	7.60	9.50	11.40	13.30	15.20	17.10	19.00
50 CENTS	1974-1978	10.30	925	9.50	0.31	.31	.62	1.24	1.86	2.48	3.10	6.20	9.30	12.40	15.50	18.60	21.70	24.80	27.90	31.00
1 DOLLAR	1974-1978	19.50	925	18.00	0.58	.58	1.16	2.32	3.48	4.64	5.80	11.60	17.40	23.20	29.00	34.80	40.60	46.40	52.20	58.00
5 DOLLARS	1974-1978	26.70	925	24.70	0.79	.79	1.58	3.16	4.74	6.32	7.90	15.80	23.70	31.60	39.50	47.40	55.30	63.20	71.10	79.00
10 DOLLARS	1974-1978	29.80	925	27.60	0.88	.88	1.76	3.52	5.28	7.04	8.80	17.60	26.40	35.20	44.00	52.80	61.60	70.40	79.20	88.00
25 DOLLARS	1978-1979	27.30	925	25.20	0.81	.81	1.62	3.24	4.86	6.48	8.10	16.20	24.30	32.40	40.50	48.60	56.70	64.80	72.90	81.00
BENIN {DAHOMEY}																				
100 FRANCS	1971	5.10	999	5.10	0.16	.16	.32	.64	.96	1.28	1.60	3.20	4.80	6.40	8.00	9.60	11.20	12.80	14.40	16.00
200 FRANCS	1971	10.30	999	10.30	0.33	.33	.66	1.32	1.98	2.64	3.30	6.60	9.90	13.20	16.50	19.80	23.10	26.40	29.70	33.00
500 FRANCS	1971	25.70	999	25.70	0.83	.83	1.66	3.28	4.92	6.56	8.30	16.60	24.90	32.80	41.50	49.20	58.10	65.60	74.70	83.00
1000 FRANCS	1971	51.50	999	51.50	1.66	1.66	3.32	6.64	9.96	13.28	16.60	33.20	49.80	66.40	83.00	99.60	116.20	132.80	149.40	166.00
BERMUDA																				
1 CROWN	1959	28.30	925	26.20	0.84	.84	1.68	3.36	5.04	6.72	8.40	16.80	25.20	33.60	42.00	50.40	58.80	67.20	75.60	84.00
1 CROWN	1964	22.60	500	11.30	0.36	.36	.72	1.44	2.16	2.88	3.60	7.20	10.80	14.40	18.00	21.60	25.20	28.80	32.40	36.00
1 DOLLAR	1970	28.60	800	22.90	0.74	.74	1.48	2.96	4.44	5.92	7.40	14.80	22.20	29.60	37.00	44.40	51.80	59.20	66.60	74.00
1 DOLLAR	1972	28.30	500	14.10	0.45	.45	.90	1.80	2.70	3.60	4.50	9.00	13.50	18.00	22.50	27.00	31.50	36.00	40.50	45.00

Coin Denomination	Years of Issue	Coin Wt. Grams	Purity	Silver Wt. Grams	Silver Troy Oz.	Silver Value—U.S. Dollars														
						$1	$2	$4	$6	$8	$10	$20	$30	$40	$50	$60	$70	$80	$90	$100
BERMUDA - CONT'D.																				
1 DOLLAR	1972	28.30	925	26.20	0.84	.84	1.68	3.36	5.04	6.72	8.40	16.80	25.20	33.60	42.00	50.40	58.80	67.20	75.60	84.00
25 DOLLARS	1975-1977	48.30	925	44.70	1.44	1.44	2.88	5.76	8.64	11.52	14.40	28.80	43.20	57.60	72.00	86.40	100.80	115.20	129.60	144.00
BHUTAN																				
3 RUPEES	1966	28.30	925	26.20	0.84	.84	1.68	3.36	5.04	6.72	8.40	16.80	25.20	33.60	42.00	50.40	58.80	67.20	75.60	84.00
15 NGUL-TRUMS	1974	22.50	500	11.30	0.36	.36	.72	1.44	2.16	2.88	3.60	7.20	10.80	14.40	18.00	21.60	25.20	28.80	32.40	36.00
30 NGUL-TRUMS	1975	22.50	500	11.30	0.36	.36	.72	1.44	2.16	2.88	3.60	7.20	10.80	14.40	18.00	21.60	25.20	28.80	32.40	36.00
BOLIVIA																				
5 CENTAVOS	1872-1900	1.30	900	1.10	0.04	.04	.08	.16	.24	.32	.40	.80	1.20	1.60	2.00	2.40	2.80	3.20	3.60	4.00
10 CENTAVOS	1872-1900	2.50	900	2.30	0.07	.07	.14	.28	.42	.56	.70	1.40	2.10	2.80	3.50	4.20	4.90	5.60	6.30	7.00
20 CENTAVOS	1872-1907	5.00	900	4.50	0.14	.14	.28	.56	.84	1.12	1.40	2.80	4.20	5.60	7.00	8.40	9.80	11.20	12.60	14.00
20 CENTAVOS	1909	5.00	833	4.20	0.14	.14	.28	.56	.84	1.12	1.40	2.80	4.20	5.60	7.00	8.40	9.80	11.20	12.60	14.00
50 CENTAVOS	1873-1908	12.50	900	11.30	0.36	.36	.72	1.44	2.16	2.88	3.60	7.20	10.80	14.40	18.00	21.60	25.20	28.80	32.40	36.00
50 CENTAVOS	1909	12.50	833	10.40	0.33	.33	.66	1.32	1.98	2.64	3.30	6.60	9.90	13.20	16.50	19.80	23.10	26.40	29.70	33.00
1 PESO	1864-1893	25.00	900	22.50	0.72	.72	1.44	2.88	4.32	5.76	7.20	14.40	21.60	28.80	36.00	43.20	50.40	57.60	64.80	72.00
100 PESOS	1975	10.00	933	9.30	0.30	.30	.60	1.20	1.80	2.40	3.00	6.00	9.00	12.00	15.00	18.00	21.00	24.00	27.00	30.00
250 PESOS	1975	15.00	933	14.00	0.45	.45	.90	1.80	2.70	3.60	4.50	9.00	13.50	18.00	22.50	27.00	31.50	36.00	40.50	45.00
500 PESOS	1975	22.00	933	20.60	0.66	.66	1.32	2.64	3.96	5.28	6.60	13.20	19.80	26.40	33.00	39.60	46.20	52.80	59.40	66.00
BOTSWANA																				
50 CENTS	1966	10.00	800	8.00	0.26	.26	.52	1.04	1.56	2.08	2.60	5.20	7.80	10.40	13.00	15.60	18.20	20.80	23.40	26.00
5 PULA	1976-1978	28.50	500	14.30	0.46	.46	.92	1.84	2.76	3.68	4.60	9.20	13.80	18.40	23.00	27.60	32.20	36.80	41.40	46.00
5 PULA	1976-1978	28.50	925	26.40	0.85	.85	1.70	3.40	5.10	6.80	8.50	17.00	25.50	34.00	42.50	51.00	59.50	68.00	76.50	85.00
10 PULA	1978	35.60	500	17.80	0.57	.57	1.14	2.28	3.42	4.56	5.70	11.40	17.10	22.80	28.50	34.20	39.90	45.60	51.30	57.00
10 PULA	1978	35.60	925	32.90	1.06	1.06	2.12	4.24	6.36	8.48	10.60	21.20	31.80	42.40	53.00	63.60	74.20	84.80	95.40	106.00
BRAZIL																				
400 REIS	1900	4.00	900	3.60	0.12	.12	.24	.48	.72	.96	1.20	2.40	3.60	4.80	6.00	7.20	8.40	9.60	10.80	12.00
500 REIS	1906-1913	5.00	900	4.50	0.14	.14	.28	.56	.84	1.12	1.40	2.80	4.20	5.60	7.00	8.40	9.80	11.20	12.60	14.00
1000 REIS	1906-1913	10.00	900	9.00	0.29	.29	.58	1.16	1.74	2.32	2.90	5.80	8.70	11.60	14.50	17.40	18.90	23.20	26.10	29.00
2000 REIS	1906-1913	20.00	900	18.00	0.58	.58	1.16	2.32	3.48	4.64	5.80	11.60	17.40	23.20	29.00	34.80	40.60	46.40	52.20	58.00
2000 REIS	1924-1935	7.50	500	3.80	0.12	.12	.24	.48	.72	.96	1.20	2.40	3.60	4.80	6.00	7.20	8.40	9.60	10.80	12.00

Coin Denomination	Years of Issue	Coin Wt. Grams	Purity	Silver Wt. Grams	Silver Troy Oz.	Silver Value—U.S. Dollars														
						$1	$2	$4	$6	$8	$10	$20	$30	$40	$50	$60	$70	$80	$90	$100
BRAZIL - CONT'D.																				
5000 REIS	1936-1938	10.00	600	6.00	0.19	.19	.38	.76	1.14	1.52	1.90	3.80	5.70	7.60	9.50	11.40	13.30	15.20	17.10	19.00
10 CRUZEIROS	1975	11.50	800	9.20	0.30	.30	.60	1.20	1.80	2.40	3.00	6.00	9.00	12.00	15.00	18.00	21.00	24.00	27.00	30.00
20 CRUZEIROS	1972	18.00	900	16.20	0.52	.52	1.04	2.08	3.12	4.16	5.20	10.40	15.60	20.80	26.00	31.20	36.40	41.60	46.80	52.00
BRITISH VIRGIN ISLANDS																				
1 CENT	1977	1.50	925	1.40	0.05	.05	.10	.20	.30	.40	.50	1.00	1.50	2.00	2.50	3.00	3.50	4.00	4.50	5.00
5 CENTS	1977	3.00	925	2.80	0.09	.09	.18	.36	.54	.72	.90	1.80	2.70	3.60	4.50	5.40	6.30	7.20	8.10	9.00
10 CENTS	1977	6.50	925	6.00	0.19	.19	.38	.76	1.14	1.52	1.90	3.80	5.70	7.60	9.50	11.40	13.30	15.20	17.10	19.00
25 CENTS	1977	7.50	925	7.10	0.23	.23	.46	.92	1.38	1.84	2.30	4.60	6.90	9.20	11.50	13.80	16.10	18.40	20.70	23.00
50 CENTS	1977	15.50	925	14.30	0.46	.46	.92	1.84	2.76	3.68	4.60	9.20	13.80	18.40	23.00	27.60	32.20	36.80	41.40	46.00
1 DOLLAR	1973-1979	28.30	925	26.20	0.84	.84	1.68	3.36	5.04	6.72	8.40	16.80	25.20	33.60	42.00	50.40	58.80	67.20	75.60	84.00
5 DOLLARS	1979	29.80	925	27.60	0.89	.89	1.78	3.56	5.34	7.12	8.90	17.80	26.70	35.60	44.50	53.40	62.30	71.20	80.10	89.00
25 DOLLARS	1979	27.30	925	25.20	0.81	.81	1.62	3.24	4.86	6.48	8.10	16.20	24.30	32.40	40.50	48.60	56.70	64.80	72.90	81.00
BRITISH WEST AFRICA																				
3 PENCE	1913-1919	1.50	925	1.40	0.05	.05	.10	.20	.30	.40	.50	1.00	1.50	2.00	2.50	3.00	3.50	4.00	4.50	5.00
3 PENCE	1920	1.50	500	0.80	0.03	.03	.06	.12	.18	.24	.30	.60	.90	1.20	1.50	1.80	2.10	2.40	2.70	3.00
6 PENCE	1913-1919	2.80	925	2.60	0.08	.08	.16	.32	.48	.64	.80	1.60	2.40	3.20	4.00	4.80	5.60	6.40	7.20	8.00
6 PENCE	1920	2.80	500	1.40	0.05	.05	.10	.20	.30	.40	.50	1.00	1.50	2.00	2.50	3.00	3.50	4.00	4.50	5.00
1 SHILLING	1913-1936	5.60	925	5.20	0.17	.17	.34	.68	1.02	1.36	1.70	3.40	5.10	6.80	8.50	10.20	11.90	13.60	15.30	17.00
2 SHILLINGS	1913-1920	11.30	925	10.50	0.34	.34	.68	1.36	2.04	2.72	3.40	6.80	10.20	13.60	17.00	20.40	23.80	27.20	30.60	34.00
2 SHILLINGS	1920	11.30	500	5.70	0.18	.18	.36	.72	1.08	1.44	1.80	3.60	5.40	7.20	9.00	10.80	12.60	14.40	16.20	18.00
BRUNEI																				
10 DOLLARS	1977-1978	28.30	925	26.20	0.84	.84	1.68	3.36	5.04	6.72	8.40	16.80	25.20	33.60	42.00	50.40	58.80	67.20	75.60	84.00
BULGARIA																				
50 STOTINKI	1883-1916	2.50	835	2.10	0.07	.07	.14	.28	.42	.56	.70	1.40	2.10	2.80	3.50	4.20	4.90	5.60	6.30	7.00
1 LIEV	1882-1916	5.00	835	4.20	0.14	.14	.28	.56	.84	1.12	1.40	2.80	4.20	5.60	7.00	8.40	9.80	11.20	12.60	14.00
2 LIEVA	1882-1916	10.00	835	8.35	0.27	.27	.54	1.08	1.62	2.16	2.70	5.40	8.10	10.80	13.50	16.20	18.90	21.60	24.30	27.00
2 LIEVA	1963-1964	8.90	900	8.00	0.26	.26	.52	1.04	1.56	2.08	2.60	5.20	7.80	10.40	13.00	15.60	18.20	20.80	23.40	26.00
5 LIEVA	1884-1894	25.00	900	22.50	0.72	.72	1.44	2.88	4.32	5.76	7.20	14.40	21.60	28.80	36.00	43.20	50.40	57.60	64.80	72.00
5 LIEVA	1963-1964	11.00	900	9.90	0.32	.32	.64	1.28	1.92	2.56	3.20	6.40	9.60	12.80	16.00	19.20	22.40	25.60	28.80	32.00
5 LIEVA	1970-1976	20.50	900	18.50	0.59	.59	1.18	2.36	3.54	4.72	5.90	11.80	17.70	23.60	29.50	35.40	41.30	47.20	53.10	59.00

Coin Denomination	Years of Issue	Coin Wt. Grams	Purity	Silver Wt. Grams	Silver Troy Oz.	Silver Value—U.S. Dollars $1	$2	$4	$6	$8	$10	$20	$30	$40	$50	$60	$70	$80	$90	$100
BULGARIA - CONT'D.																				
5 LIEVA	1976-1978	20.50	500	10.30	0.33	.33	.66	1.32	1.98	2.64	3.30	6.60	9.90	13.20	16.50	19.80	23.10	26.40	29.70	33.00
10 LIEVA	1975	30.20	900	27.20	0.87	.87	1.74	3.48	5.22	6.96	8.70	17.40	26.10	34.80	43.50	52.20	60.90	69.60	78.30	87.00
10 LIEVA	1978	30.20	500	15.10	0.49	.49	.98	1.96	2.94	3.92	4.90	9.80	14.70	19.60	24.50	29.40	34.30	39.20	44.10	49.00
20 LIEVA	1979	32.00	900	28.80	0.93	.93	1.86	3.72	5.58	7.74	9.30	18.60	27.90	37.20	46.50	55.80	65.10	74.40	83.70	93.00
20 LIEVA	1930	4.00	500	2.00	0.06	.06	.12	.24	.36	.48	.60	1.20	1.80	2.40	3.00	3.60	4.20	4.80	5.40	6.00
50 LIEVA	1930-1934	10.00	500	5.00	0.16	.16	.32	.64	.96	1.28	1.60	3.20	4.80	6.40	8.00	9.60	11.20	12.80	14.40	16.00
100 LIEVA	1930-1937	20.00	500	10.00	0.32	.32	.64	1.28	1.92	2.56	3.20	6.40	9.60	12.80	16.00	19.20	22.40	25.60	28.80	32.00
CANADA																				
5 CENTS	1858-1917	1.16	925	1.10	0.04	.04	.08	.16	.24	.32	.40	.80	1.20	1.60	2.00	2.40	2.80	3.20	3.60	4.00
5 CENTS	1920-1921	1.16	800	0.90	0.03	.03	.06	.12	.18	.24	.30	.60	.90	1.20	1.50	1.80	2.10	2.40	2.70	3.00
10 CENTS	1858-1917	2.30	925	2.20	0.07	.07	.14	.28	.42	.56	.70	1.40	2.10	2.80	3.50	4.20	4.90	5.60	6.30	7.00
10 CENTS	1920-1967	2.30	800	1.90	0.06	.06	.12	.24	.36	.48	.60	1.20	1.80	2.40	3.00	3.60	4.20	4.80	5.40	6.00
10 CENTS	1967	2.30	500	1.20	0.04	.04	.08	.16	.24	.32	.40	.80	1.20	1.60	2.00	2.40	2.80	3.20	3.60	4.00
25 CENTS	1870-1919	5.80	925	5.40	0.17	.17	.34	.68	1.02	1.36	1.70	3.40	5.10	6.80	8.50	10.20	11.90	13.60	15.30	17.00
25 CENTS	1920-1967	5.80	800	4.60	0.15	.15	.30	.60	.90	1.20	1.50	3.00	4.50	6.00	7.50	9.00	10.50	12.00	13.50	15.00
25 CENTS	1967	5.80	500	2.90	0.09	.09	.18	.36	.54	.72	.90	1.80	2.70	3.60	4.50	5.40	6.30	7.20	8.10	9.00
50 CENTS	1870-1919	11.60	925	10.70	0.34	.34	.68	1.36	2.04	2.72	3.40	6.80	10.20	13.60	17.00	20.40	23.80	27.20	30.60	34.00
50 CENTS	1920-1967	11.60	800	9.30	0.30	.30	.60	1.20	1.80	2.40	3.00	6.00	9.00	12.00	15.00	18.00	21.00	24.00	27.00	30.00
1 DOLLAR	1935-1967	23.30	800	18.70	0.60	.60	1.20	2.40	3.60	4.80	6.00	12.00	18.00	24.00	30.00	36.00	42.00	48.00	54.00	60.00
1 DOLLAR	1971-1978	23.50	500	11.70	0.38	.38	.76	1.52	2.28	3.04	3.80	7.60	11.40	15.20	19.00	22.80	26.60	30.40	34.20	38.00
5 DOLLARS	1973-1976	24.30	925	22.50	0.72	.72	1.44	2.88	4.32	5.76	7.20	14.40	21.60	28.80	36.00	43.20	50.40	57.60	64.80	72.00
10 DOLLARS	1973-1976	48.60	925	45.00	1.45	1.45	2.90	5.80	8.70	11.60	14.50	29.00	43.50	58.00	72.50	87.00	101.50	116.00	130.50	145.00
CAPE VERDE																				
10 ESCUDOS	1953	10.00	720	7.20	0.23	.23	.46	.92	1.38	1.84	2.30	4.60	6.90	9.20	11.50	13.80	16.10	18.40	20.70	23.00
250 ESCUDOS	1976	16.70	900	15.00	0.48	.48	.96	1.92	2.88	3.84	4.80	9.60	14.40	19.20	24.00	28.80	33.60	38.40	43.20	48.00
CAYMAN ISLANDS																				
50 CENTS	1972-1978	10.60	925	9.80	0.32	.32	.64	1.28	1.92	2.56	3.20	6.40	9.60	12.80	16.00	19.20	22.40	25.60	28.80	32.00
1 DOLLAR	1972-1978	18.40	925	17.00	0.55	.55	1.10	2.20	3.30	4.40	5.50	11.00	16.50	22.00	27.50	33.00	38.50	44.00	49.50	55.00
2 DOLLARS	1972-1978	29.90	925	26.70	0.86	.86	1.72	3.44	5.16	6.88	8.60	17.20	25.80	34.40	43.00	51.60	60.20	68.80	77.40	86.00
5 DOLLARS	1972-1978	35.90	925	33.20	1.07	1.07	2.14	4.28	6.42	8.56	10.70	21.40	32.10	42.80	53.50	64.20	74.90	85.60	96.30	107.00
25 DOLLARS	1972-1978	51.50	925	47.60	1.53	1.53	3.06	6.12	9.18	12.24	15.30	30.60	45.90	61.20	76.50	91.80	107.10	122.40	137.70	153.00
50 DOLLARS	1975-1978	64.90	925	60.10	1.93	1.93	3.86	7.72	11.58	15.44	19.30	38.60	57.90	77.20	96.50	115.80	135.10	154.40	173.70	193.00

Coin Denomination	Years of Issue	Coin Wt. Grams	Purity	Silver Wt. Grams	Silver Troy Oz.	Silver Value—U.S. Dollars $1	$2	$4	$6	$8	$10	$20	$30	$40	$50	$60	$70	$80	$90	$100
CHAD																				
100 FRANCS	1970	3.20	925	3.00	0.10	.10	.20	.40	.60	.80	1.00	2.00	3.00	4.00	5.00	6.00	7.00	8.00	9.00	10.00
200 FRANCS	1970	9.70	925	9.00	0.29	.29	.58	1.16	1.74	2.32	2.90	5.80	8.70	11.60	14.50	17.40	18.90	23.20	26.10	29.00
300 FRANCS	1970	16.10	925	14.90	0.48	.48	.96	1.92	2.88	3.84	4.80	9.60	14.40	19.20	24.00	28.80	33.60	38.40	43.20	48.00
CEYLON {SRI LANKA}																				
10 CENTS	1892-1917	1.20	800	.90	0.03	.03	.06	.12	.18	.24	.30	.60	.90	1.20	1.50	1.80	2.10	2.40	2.70	3.00
10 CENTS	1919-1928	1.20	550	.60	0.02	.02	.04	.08	.12	.16	.20	.40	.60	.80	1.00	1.20	1.40	1.60	1.80	2.00
25 CENTS	1892-1917	2.90	800	2.30	0.07	.07	.14	.28	.42	.56	.70	1.40	2.10	2.80	3.50	4.20	4.90	5.60	6.30	7.00
25 CENTS	1919-1926	2.90	550	1.60	0.05	.05	.10	.20	.30	.40	.50	1.00	1.50	2.00	2.50	3.00	3.50	4.00	4.50	5.00
50 CENTS	1892-1917	5.80	800	4.70	0.15	.15	.30	.60	.90	1.20	1.50	3.00	4.50	6.00	7.50	9.00	10.50	12.00	13.50	15.00
50 CENTS	1919-1929	5.80	550	3.20	0.10	.10	.20	.40	.60	.80	1.00	2.00	3.00	4.00	5.00	6.00	7.00	8.00	9.00	10.00
5 RUPEES	1957	28.30	925	26.20	0.84	.84	1.68	3.36	5.04	6.72	8.40	16.80	25.20	33.60	42.00	50.40	58.80	67.20	75.60	84.00
CHILE																				
1/2 DECIMO	1851-1881	1.20	900	1.10	0.04	.04	.08	.16	.24	.32	.40	.80	1.20	1.60	2.00	2.40	2.80	3.20	3.60	4.00
1/2 DECIMO	1879-1894	1.20	500	0.60	0.02	.02	.04	.08	.12	.16	.20	.40	.60	.80	1.00	1.20	1.40	1.60	1.80	2.00
1 DECIMO	1852-1880	2.00	900	1.80	0.06	.06	.12	.24	.36	.48	.60	1.20	1.80	2.40	3.00	3.60	4.20	4.80	5.40	6.00
1 DECIMO	1879-1894	2.00	500	1.00	0.03	.03	.06	.12	.18	.24	.30	.60	.90	1.20	1.50	1.80	2.10	2.40	2.70	3.00
5 CENTAVOS	1896	1.25	835	1.00	0.03	.03	.06	.12	.18	.24	.30	.60	.90	1.20	1.50	1.80	2.10	2.40	2.70	3.00
5 CENTAVOS	1899-1907	1.30	500	0.60	0.02	.02	.04	.08	.12	.16	.20	.40	.60	.80	1.00	1.20	1.40	1.60	1.80	2.00
5 CENTAVOS	1908-1919	1.00	400	0.40	0.01	.01	.02	.04	.06	.08	.10	.20	.30	.40	.50	.60	.70	.80	.90	1.00
10 CENTAVOS	1896	2.50	835	2.10	0.07	.07	.14	.28	.42	.56	.70	1.40	2.10	2.80	3.50	4.20	4.90	5.60	6.30	7.00
10 CENTRAVOS	1899-1907	2.50	500	1.30	0.04	.04	.08	.16	.24	.32	.40	.80	1.20	1.60	2.00	2.40	2.80	3.20	3.60	4.00
10 CENTAVOS	1908-1920	1.50	400	0.60	0.02	.02	.04	.08	.12	.16	.20	.40	.60	.80	1.00	1.20	1.40	1.60	1.80	2.00
20 CENTAVOS	1852-1879	5.00	900	4.50	0.14	.14	.28	.56	.84	1.12	1.40	2.80	4.20	5.60	7.00	8.40	9.80	11.20	12.60	14.00
20 CENTAVOS	1895	5.00	835	4.20	0.14	.14	.28	.56	.84	1.12	1.40	2.80	4.20	5.60	7.00	8.40	9.80	11.20	12.60	14.00
20 CENTAVOS	1879-1907	5.00	500	2.50	0.08	.08	.16	.32	.48	.64	.80	1.60	2.40	3.20	4.00	4.80	5.60	6.40	7.20	8.00
20 CENTAVOS	1916	5.00	450	2.30	0.07	.07	.14	.28	.42	.56	.70	1.40	2.10	2.80	3.50	4.20	4.90	5.60	6.30	7.00
20 CENTAVOS	1907-1920	5.00	400	3.20	0.10	.10	.20	.40	.60	.80	1.00	2.00	3.00	4.00	5.00	6.00	7.00	8.00	9.00	10.00
20 CENTAVOS	1891	4.00	500	2.00	0.06	.06	.12	.24	.36	.48	.60	1.20	1.80	2.40	3.00	3.60	4.20	4.80	5.40	6.00
20 CENTAVOS	1891	5.00	200	1.00	0.03	.03	.06	.12	.18	.24	.30	.60	.90	1.20	1.50	1.80	2.10	2.40	2.70	3.00
40 CENTAVOS	1907-1908	8.00	400	3.20	0.10	.10	.20	.40	.60	.80	1.00	2.00	3.00	4.00	5.00	6.00	7.00	8.00	9.00	10.00
50 CENTAVOS	1853-1872	10.00	900	9.00	0.29	.29	.58	1.16	1.74	2.32	2.90	5.80	8.70	11.60	14.50	17.40	18.90	23.20	26.10	29.00
50 CENTAVOS	1902-1906	10.00	700	7.00	0.23	.23	.46	.92	1.38	1.84	2.30	4.60	6.90	9.20	11.50	13.80	16.10	18.40	20.70	23.00
1 PESO	1853-1891	25.00	900	22.50	0.72	.72	1.44	2.88	4.32	5.76	7.20	14.40	21.60	28.80	36.00	43.20	50.40	57.60	64.80	72.00
1 PESO	1895-1897	20.00	835	16.70	0.54	.54	1.08	2.16	3.24	4.32	5.40	10.80	16.20	21.60	27.00	32.40	37.80	43.20	48.60	54.00
1 PESO	1902-1905	20.00	700	14.00	0.45	.45	.90	1.80	2.70	3.60	4.50	9.00	13.50	18.00	22.50	27.00	31.50	36.00	40.50	45.00
1 PESO	1910	20.00	900	18.00	0.58	.58	1.16	2.32	3.48	4.64	5.80	11.60	17.40	23.20	29.00	34.80	40.60	46.40	52.20	58.00
1 PESO	1915-1917	9.00	720	6.50	0.21	.21	.42	.84	1.26	1.68	2.10	4.20	6.30	8.40	10.50	12.60	14.70	16.80	18.90	21.00
1 PESO	1921-1927	9.00	500	4.50	0.14	.14	.28	.56	.84	1.12	1.40	2.80	4.20	5.60	7.00	8.40	9.80	11.20	12.60	14.00

Coin Denomination	Years of Issue	Coin Wt. Grams	Purity	Silver Wt. Grams	Silver Troy Oz.	Silver Value—U.S. Dollars														
						$1	$2	$4	$6	$8	$10	$20	$30	$40	$50	$60	$70	$80	$90	$100
CHILE - CONT'D.																				
1 PESO	1932	6.00	400	2.40	0.08	.08	.16	.32	.48	.64	.80	1.60	2.40	3.20	4.00	4.80	5.60	6.40	7.20	8.00
2 PESOS	1927	18.00	500	9.00	0.29	.29	.58	1.16	1.74	2.32	2.90	5.80	8.70	11.60	14.50	17.40	18.90	23.20	26.10	29.00
5 PESOS	1927	25.00	900	22.50	0.72	.72	1.44	2.88	4.32	5.76	7.20	14.40	21.60	28.80	36.00	43.20	50.40	57.60	64.80	72.00
5 PESOS	1968	22.10	1000	22.10	0.71	.71	1.42	2.84	4.26	5.68	7.10	14.20	21.30	28.40	35.50	42.60	49.70	56.80	63.90	71.00
10 PESOS	1968	44.50	1000	44.50	0.43	.43	.86	1.72	2.58	3.44	4.30	8.60	12.90	17.20	21.50	25.80	30.10	34.40	38.70	43.00
CHTNA																				
1 YUAN	1912-1934	26.80	900	24.10	0.77	.77	1.54	3.08	4.62	6.16	7.70	15.40	23.10	30.80	38.50	46.20	53.90	61.60	69.30	77.00
CHINA, NATIONALIST																				
50 DOLLARS	1965	17.50	750	13.10	0.42	.42	.84	1.68	2.52	3.36	4.20	8.40	12.60	16.80	21.00	25.20	29.40	33.60	37.80	42.00
100 DOLLARS	1965	22.50	750	16.90	0.54	.54	1.08	2.16	3.24	4.32	5.40	10.80	16.20	21.60	27.00	32.40	37.80	43.20	48.60	54.00
COLUMBIA																				
10 CENTAVOS	1872-1885	2.50	835	2.10	0.07	.07	.14	.28	.42	.56	.70	1.40	2.10	2.80	3.50	4.20	4.90	5.60	6.30	7.00
10 CENTAVOS	1885-1886	2.50	500	1.30	0.04	.04	.08	.16	.24	.32	.40	.80	1.20	1.60	2.00	2.40	2.80	3.20	3.60	4.00
10 CENTAVOS	1885-1886	2.50	835	2.10	0.07	.07	.14	.28	.42	.56	.70	1.40	2.10	2.80	3.50	4.20	4.90	5.60	6.30	7.00
10 CENTAVOS	1897	2.50	666	1.70	0.05	.05	.10	.20	.30	.40	.50	1.00	1.50	2.00	2.50	3.00	3.50	4.00	4.50	5.00
10 CENTAVOS	1911-1942	2.50	900	2.30	0.07	.07	.14	.28	.42	.56	.70	1.40	2.10	2.80	3.50	4.20	4.90	5.60	6.30	7.00
10 CENTAVOS	1945-1952	2.50	500	1.30	0.04	.04	.08	.16	.24	.32	.40	.80	1.20	1.60	2.00	2.40	2.80	3.20	3.60	4.00
20 CENTAVOS	1886	5.00	500	2.50	0.08	.08	.16	.32	.48	.64	.80	1.60	2.40	3.20	4.00	4.80	5.60	6.40	7.20	8.00
20 CENTAVOS	1874-1886	5.00	835	4.20	0.14	.14	.28	.56	.84	1.12	1.40	2.80	4.20	5.60	7.00	8.40	9.80	11.20	12.60	14.00
20 CENTAVOS	1897	5.00	666	3.30	0.11	.11	.22	.44	.66	.88	1.10	2.20	3.30	4.40	.50	6.60	7.70	8.80	9.90	11.00
20 CENTAVOS	1911-1942	5.00	900	4.50	0.14	.14	.28	.56	.84	1.12	1.40	2.80	4.20	5.60	7.00	8.40	9.80	11.20	12.60	14.00
20 CENTAVOS	1945-1952	5.00	500	2.50	0.08	.08	.16	.32	.48	.64	.80	1.60	2.40	3.20	4.00	4.80	5.60	6.40	7.20	8.00
20 CENTAVOS	1953	5.00	300	1.50	0.05	.05	.10	.20	.30	.40	.50	1.00	1.50	2.00	2.50	3.00	3.50	4.00	4.50	5.00
50 CENTAVOS	1872-1873	12.50	500	6.00	0.19	.19	.38	.76	1.14	1.52	1.90	3.80	5.70	7.60	9.50	11.40	13.30	15.20	17.10	19.00
50 CENTAVOS	1872-1902	12.50	835	10.40	0.33	.33	.66	1.32	1.98	2.64	3.30	6.60	9.90	13.20	16.50	19.80	23.10	26.40	29.70	33.00
50 CENTAVOS	1912-1934	12.50	900	11.30	0.36	.36	.72	1.44	2.16	2.88	3.60	7.20	10.80	14.40	18.00	21.60	25.20	28.80	32.40	36.00
50 CENTAVOS	1947-1948	12.50	500	6.30	0.20	.20	.40	.80	1.20	1.60	2.00	4.00	6.00	8.00	10.00	12.00	14.00	16.00	18.00	20.00
1 PESO	1956	25.00	900	22.50	0.72	.72	1.44	2.88	4.32	5.76	7.20	14.40	21.60	28.80	37.00	43.20	50.40	57.60	64.80	72.00
300 PESOS	1979	28.30	925	26.20	0.84	.84	1.68	3.36	5.04	6.72	8.40	16.80	25.20	33.60	42.00	50.40	58.80	67.20	75.60	84.00
500 PESOS	1979	35.00	925	32.40	1.04	1.04	2.08	4.16	6.24	8.32	10.40	20.80	31.20	41.60	52.00	62.40	72.80	83.20	93.60	104.00

Coin Denomination	Years of Issue	Coin Wt. Grams	Purity	Silver Wt. Grams	Silver Troy Oz.	$1	$2	$4	$6	$8	$10	$20	$30	$40	$50	$60	$70	$80	$90	$100
COOK ISLANDS																				
2 DOLLARS	1973	25.50	925	23.60	0.76	.76	1.52	3.04	4.56	6.08	7.60	15.20	22.80	30.40	38.00	45.60	53.20	60.80	68.40	76.00
2-1/2 DOLLAR	1973-1974	27.10	925	25.10	0.81	.81	1.62	3.24	4.86	6.48	8.10	16.20	24.30	32.40	40.50	48.60	56.70	64.80	72.90	81.00
5 DOLLARS	1976-1978	27.30	500	13.70	0.44	.44	.88	1.76	2.64	3.52	4.40	8.80	13.20	17.60	22.00	26.40	30.80	35.20	39.60	44.00
7-1/2 DOLLAR	1973-1974	34.60	925	32.00	1.03	1.03	2.06	4.12	6.18	8.24	10.30	20.60	30.90	41.20	51.50	61.80	72.10	82.40	92.70	103.00
10 DOLLARS	1978	27.30	925	25.20	0.81	.81	1.62	3.24	4.86	6.48	8.10	16.20	24.30	32.40	40.50	48.60	56.70	64.80	72.90	81.00
25 DOLLARS	1977	48.60	925	45.00	1.45	1.45	2.90	5.80	8.70	11.60	14.50	29.00	43.50	58.00	72.50	87.00	101.50	116.00	130.50	145.00
50 DOLLARS	1974	97.20	925	89.90	2.89	2.89	5.78	11.56	17.34	23.12	28.90	57.80	86.70	115.60	144.50	173.40	202.30	231.20	260.10	289.00
COSTA RICA																				
5 CENTIMOS	1905-1914	1.00	900	0.90	0.03	.03	.06	.12	.18	.24	.30	.60	.90	1.20	1.50	1.80	2.10	2.40	2.70	3.00
10 CENTIMOS	1905-1914	2.00	900	1.80	0.06	.06	.12	.24	.36	.48	.60	1.20	1.80	2.40	3.00	3.60	4.20	4.80	5.40	6.00
10 CENTAVOS	1917	2.00	500	1.00	0.03	.03	.06	.12	.18	.24	.30	.60	.90	1.20	1.50	1.80	2.10	2.40	2.70	3.00
25 CENTIMOS	1924	3.25	650	2.10	0.07	.07	.14	.28	.42	.56	.70	1.40	2.10	2.80	3.50	4.20	4.90	5.60	6.30	7.00
50 CENTIMOS	1902-1914	10.00	900	9.00	0.29	.29	.58	1.16	1.74	2.32	2.90	5.80	8.70	11.60	14.50	17.40	18.90	23.20	26.10	29.00
50 CENTIMOS	1917-1918	10.00	500	5.00	0.16	.16	.32	.64	.96	1.28	1.60	3.20	4.80	6.40	8.00	9.60	11.20	12.80	14.40	16.00
2 COLONES	1970	4.30	1000	4.30	0.14	.14	.28	.56	.84	1.12	1.40	2.80	4.20	5.60	7.00	8.40	9.80	11.20	12.60	14.00
5 COLONES	1970	10.80	1000	10.80	0.35	.35	.70	1.40	2.10	2.80	3.50	7.00	10.50	14.00	17.50	21.00	24.50	28.00	31.50	35.00
10 COLONES	1970	21.60	1000	21.60	0.69	.69	1.38	2.76	4.14	5.52	6.90	13.80	20.70	27.60	34.50	41.40	48.30	55.20	62.10	69.00
20 COLONES	1970	43.10	1000	43.10	1.39	1.39	2.78	5.56	8.34	11.12	13.90	27.80	41.70	55.60	69.50	83.40	97.30	111.20	125.10	139.00
25 COLONES	1970	53.90	1000	53.90	1.73	1.73	3.46	6.92	10.38	13.84	17.30	34.60	51.90	69.20	86.50	103.80	121.10	138.40	155.70	173.00
50 COLONES	1974	25.30	500	12.70	0.41	.41	.82	1.64	2.46	3.28	4.10	8.20	12.30	16.40	20.50	24.60	28.70	32.80	36.90	41.00
50 COLONES	1974	28.30	925	26.20	0.84	.84	1.68	3.36	5.04	6.72	8.40	16.80	25.20	33.60	42.00	50.40	58.80	67.20	75.60	84.00
100 COLONES	1974	31.70	500	15.80	0.51	.51	1.02	2.04	3.06	4.08	5.10	10.20	15.30	20.40	25.50	30.60	35.70	40.80	45.90	51.00
100 COLONES	1974	35.00	925	32.40	1.04	1.04	2.08	4.16	6.24	8.32	10.40	20.80	31.20	41.60	52.00	62.40	72.80	83.20	93.60	104.00
CUBA																				
10 CENTAVOS	1915-1952	2.50	900	2.30	0.07	.07	.14	.28	.42	.56	.70	1.40	2.10	2.80	3.50	4.20	4.90	5.60	6.30	7.00
20 CENTAVOS	1915-1952	5.00	900	4.50	0.14	.14	.28	.56	.84	1.12	1.40	2.80	4.20	5.60	7.00	8.40	9.80	11.20	12.60	14.00
25 CENTAVOS	1953	6.70	900	6.00	0.19	.19	.38	.76	1.14	1.52	1.90	3.80	5.70	7.60	9.50	11.40	13.30	15.20	17.10	19.00
40 CENTAVOS	1915-1952	10.00	900	9.00	0.29	.29	.58	1.16	1.74	2.32	2.90	5.80	8.70	11.60	14.50	17.40	18.90	23.20	26.10	29.00
50 CENTAVOS	1915-1953	26.70	900	24.10	0.77	.77	1.54	3.08	4.62	6.16	7.70	15.40	23.10	30.80	38.50	46.20	53.90	61.60	69.30	77.00
1 PESO	1915-1953	26.70	900	24.10	0.77	.77	1.54	3.08	4.62	6.16	7.70	15.40	23.10	30.80	38.50	46.20	53.90	61.60	69.30	77.00
5 PESOS	1975	13.30	900	12.00	0.39	.39	.78	1.56	2.34	3.12	3.90	7.80	11.70	15.60	19.50	23.40	27.30	31.20	35.10	39.00
10 PESOS	1975	26.70	900	24.00	0.77	.77	1.54	3.08	4.62	6.16	7.70	15.40	23.10	30.80	38.50	46.20	53.90	61.60	69.30	77.00
CYPRUS																				
3 PIASTRES	1901	1.90	925	1.70	0.05	.05	.10	.20	.30	.40	.50	1.00	1.50	2.00	2.50	3.00	3.50	4.00	4.50	5.00
4-1/2 PIASTRES	1901-1938	2.80	925	2.60	0.08	.08	.16	.32	.48	.64	.80	1.60	2.40	3.20	4.00	4.80	5.60	6.40	7.20	8.00

Silver Value—U.S. Dollars

Coin Denomination	Years of Issue	Coin Wt. Grams	Purity	Silver Wt. Grams	Silver Troy Oz.	Silver Value—U.S. Dollars														
						$1	$2	$4	$6	$8	$10	$20	$30	$40	$50	$60	$70	$80	$90	$100
CYPRESS - CONT'D.																				
9 PIASTRES	1901-1940	5.70	925	5.20	0.17	.17	.34	.68	1.02	1.36	1.70	3.40	5.10	6.80	8.50	10.20	11.90	13.60	15.30	17.00
18 PIASTRES	1901-1940	11.30	925	10.50	0.34	.34	.68	1.36	2.04	2.72	3.40	6.80	10.20	13.60	17.00	20.40	23.80	27.20	30.60	34.00
45 PIASTRES	1928	28.30	925	26.20	0.84	.84	1.68	3.36	5.04	6.72	8.40	16.80	25.20	33.60	42.00	50.40	58.80	67.20	75.60	84.00
500 MILS	1970	22.60	800	18.20	0.59	.59	1.18	2.36	3.54	4.72	5.90	11.80	17.70	23.60	29.50	35.40	41.30	47.20	53.10	59.00
500 MILS	1975	14.10	800	11.30	0.36	.36	.72	1.44	2.16	2.88	3.60	7.20	10.80	14.40	18.00	21.60	25.20	28.80	32.40	36.00
500 MILS	1976	14.10	925	13.10	0.42	.42	.84	1.68	2.52	3.36	4.20	8.40	12.60	16.80	21.00	25.20	29.40	33.60	37.80	42.00
1 POUND	1976	28.50	925	26.30	0.85	.85	1.70	3.40	5.10	6.80	8.50	17.00	25.50	34.00	42.50	51.00	59.50	68.00	76.50	85.00
CZECHOSLOVAKIA																				
5 KORUN	1928-1932	7.00	500	3.50	0.11	.11	.22	.44	.66	.88	1.10	2.20	3.30	4.40	5.50	6.60	7.70	8.80	9.90	11.00
10 KORUN	1928-1933	10.00	700	7.00	0.23	.23	.46	.92	1.38	1.84	2.30	4.60	6.90	9.20	11.50	13.80	16.10	18.40	20.70	23.00
10 KORUN	1954-1968	12.00	500	6.00	0.19	.19	.38	.76	1.14	1.52	1.90	3.80	5.70	7.60	9.50	11.40	13.30	15.20	17.10	19.00
20 KORUN	1933-1937	12.00	700	8.40	0.27	.27	.54	1.08	1.62	2.16	2.70	5.40	8.10	10.80	13.50	16.20	18.90	21.60	24.30	27.00
20 KORUN	1972	12.00	500	6.00	0.19	.19	.38	.76	1.14	1.52	1.90	3.80	5.70	7.60	9.50	11.40	13.30	15.20	17.10	19.00
25 KORUN	1954-1969	16.00	500	8.00	0.26	.26	.52	1.04	1.56	2.08	2.60	5.20	7.80	10.40	13.00	15.60	18.20	20.80	23.40	26.00
25 KORUN	1970	12.00	700	8.40	0.27	.27	.54	1.08	1.62	2.16	2.70	5.40	8.10	10.80	13.50	16.20	18.90	21.60	24.30	27.00
50 KORUN	1947-1949	10.00	500	5.00	0.16	.16	.32	.64	.96	1.28	1.60	3.20	4.80	6.40	8.00	9.60	11.20	12.80	14.40	16.00
50 KORUN	1955-1968	20.00	900	18.00	0.58	.58	1.16	2.32	3.48	4.64	5.80	11.60	17.40	23.20	29.00	34.80	40.60	46.40	52.20	58.00
50 KORUN	1970-1979	13.00	700	9.10	0.29	.29	.58	1.16	1.74	2.32	2.90	5.80	8.70	11.60	14.50	17.40	18.90	23.20	26.10	29.00
100 KORUN	1948-1951	14.00	500	7.00	0.23	.23	.46	.92	1.38	1.84	2.30	4.60	6.90	9.20	11.50	13.80	16.10	18.40	20.70	23.00
100 KORUN	1955	24.00	900	21.60	0.69	.69	1.38	2.76	4.14	5.52	6.90	13.80	20.70	27.60	34.50	41.40	48.30	55.20	62.10	69.00
100 KORUN	1971-1979	15.00	700	10.50	0.34	.34	.68	1.36	2.04	2.72	3.40	6.80	10.20	13.60	17.00	20.40	23.80	27.20	30.60	34.00
SLOVAKIA																				
10 KORUN	1944	7.50	500	3.80	0.12	.12	.24	.48	.72	.96	1.20	2.40	3.60	4.80	6.00	7.20	8.40	9.60	10.80	12.00
20 KORUN	1939-1941	15.00	500	7.50	0.24	.24	.48	.96	1.44	1.92	2.40	4.80	7.20	9.60	12.00	14.40	16.80	19.20	21.60	24.00
50 KORUN	1944	16.50	700	11.60	0.37	.37	.74	1.48	2.22	2.96	3.70	7.40	11.10	14.80	18.50	22.20	25.90	29.60	33.30	37.00
DENMARK																				
10 ORE	1874-1919	1.50	400	0.60	0.02	.02	.04	.08	.12	.16	.20	.40	.60	.80	1.00	1.20	1.40	1.60	1.80	2.00
25 ORE	1874-1919	2.40	600	1.50	0.05	.05	.10	.20	.30	.40	.50	1.00	1.50	2.00	2.50	3.00	3.50	4.00	4.50	5.00
1 KRONE	1875-1916	7.50	800	6.00	0.19	.19	.38	.76	1.14	1.52	1.90	3.80	5.70	7.60	9.50	11.40	13.30	15.20	17.10	19.00
2 KRONER	1875-1958	15.00	800	12.00	0.39	.39	.78	1.56	2.34	3.12	3.90	7.80	11.70	15.60	19.50	23.40	27.30	31.20	35.10	39.00
5 KRONER	1960-1964	17.00	800	13.60	0.44	.44	.88	1.76	2.64	3.52	4.40	8.80	13.20	17.60	22.00	26.40	30.80	35.20	39.60	44.00
10 KRONER	1967-1972	20.40	800	16.30	0.52	.52	1.04	2.08	3.12	4.16	5.20	10.40	15.60	20.80	26.00	31.20	36.40	41.60	46.80	52.00

Coin Denomination	Years of Issue	Coin Wt. Grams	Purity	Silver Wt. Grams	Silver Troy Oz.	Silver Value—U.S. Dollars														
						$1	$2	$4	$6	$8	$10	$20	$30	$40	$50	$60	$70	$80	$90	$100
DOMINICAN REPUBLIC																				
5 CENTAVOS	1944	1.30	350	0.50	0.02	.02	.04	.08	.12	.16	.20	.40	.60	.80	1.00	1.20	1.40	1.60	1.80	2.00
10 CENTAVOS	1937-1961	2.50	900	2.30	0.07	.07	.14	.28	.42	.56	.70	1.40	2.10	2.80	3.50	4.20	4.90	5.60	6.30	7.00
25 CENTAVOS	1937-1961	6.50	900	5.60	0.18	.18	.36	.72	1.08	1.44	1.80	3.60	5.40	7.20	9.00	10.80	12.60	14.40	16.20	18.00
1/2 PESO	1937-1961	12.50	900	11.30	0.36	.36	.72	1.44	2.16	2.88	3.60	7.20	10.80	14.40	18.00	21.60	25.20	28.80	32.40	36.00
1 PESO	1939-1955	26.70	900	24.00	0.77	.77	1.54	3.08	4.62	6.16	7.70	15.40	23.10	30.80	38.50	46.20	53.90	61.60	69.30	77.00
1 PESO	1963	26.70	650	17.40	0.56	.56	1.12	2.24	3.36	4.48	5.60	11.20	16.80	22.40	28.00	33.60	39.20	44.80	50.40	56.00
1 PESO	1972-1979	26.70	900	24.00	0.77	.77	1.54	3.08	4.62	6.16	7.70	15.40	23.10	30.80	38.50	46.20	53.90	61.60	69.30	77.00
10 PESOS	1975	28.00	900	25.20	0.81	.81	1.62	3.24	4.86	6.48	8.10	16.20	24.30	32.40	40.50	48.60	56.70	64.80	72.90	81.00
30 PESOS	1977	78.00	925	72.20	2.32	2.32	4.64	9.28	13.92	18.56	23.20	46.40	69.60	92.80	116.00	139.20	162.40	185.60	208.80	232.00
EAST AFRICA																				
25 CENTS	1906-1918	1.90	800	1.60	0.05	.05	.10	.20	.30	.40	.50	1.00	1.50	2.00	2.50	3.00	3.50	4.00	4.50	5.00
25 CENTS	1920	1.90	550	1.00	0.03	.03	.06	.12	.18	.24	.30	.60	.90	1.20	1.50	1.80	2.10	2.40	2.70	3.00
50 CENTS	1906-1919	3.90	800	3.10	0.10	.10	.20	.40	.60	.80	1.00	2.00	3.00	4.00	5.00	6.00	7.00	8.00	9.00	10.00
50 CENTS	1921-1944	3.80	250	1.00	0.03	.03	.06	.12	.18	.24	.30	.60	.90	1.20	1.50	1.80	2.10	2.40	2.70	3.00
1 SHILLING	1921-1946	7.80	250	1.90	0.06	.06	.12	.24	.36	.48	.60	1.20	1.80	2.40	3.00	3.60	4.20	4.80	5.40	6.00
1 FLORIN	1920	11.70	500	5.80	0.19	.19	.38	.76	1.14	1.52	1.90	3.80	5.70	7.60	9.50	11.40	13.30	15.20	17.10	19.00
ECUADOR																				
1/2 DECIMO	1893-1915	1.30	900	1.10	0.04	.04	.08	.16	.24	.32	.40	.80	1.20	1.60	2.00	2.40	2.80	3.20	3.60	4.00
1 DECIMO	1884-1916	2.50	900	2.30	0.07	.07	.14	.28	.42	.56	.70	1.40	2.10	2.80	3.50	4.20	4.90	5.60	6.30	7.00
2 DECIMOS	1884-1916	5.00	900	0.14	0.14	.14	.28	.56	.84	1.12	1.40	2.80	4.20	5.60	7.00	8.40	9.80	11.20	12.60	14.00
50 CENTAVOS	1928-1930	2.50	720	1.80	0.06	.06	.12	.24	.36	.48	.60	1.20	1.80	2.40	3.00	3.60	4.20	4.80	5.40	6.00
1 SUCRE	1884-1897	25.00	900	22.50	0.72	.72	1.44	2.88	4.32	5.76	7.20	14.40	21.60	28.80	36.00	43.20	50.40	57.60	64.80	72.00
1 SUCRE	1928-1934	5.00	720	3.60	0.12	.12	.24	.48	.72	.96	1.20	2.40	3.60	4.80	6.00	7.20	8.40	9.60	10.80	12.00
2 SUCRES	1928-1944	10.00	720	7.20	0.23	.23	.46	.92	1.38	1.84	2.30	4.60	6.90	9.20	11.50	13.80	16.10	18.40	20.70	23.00
5 SUCRES	1943-1944	25.00	720	18.00	0.58	.58	1.16	2.32	3.48	4.64	5.80	11.60	17.40	23.20	29.00	34.80	40.60	46.40	52.20	58.00
EGYPT																				
2 PIASTRES	1916-1942	2.80	833	2.30	0.07	.07	.14	.28	.42	.56	.70	1.40	2.10	2.80	3.50	4.20	4.90	5.60	6.30	7.00
2 PIASTRES	1944	2.80	625	1.80	0.06	.06	.12	.24	.36	.48	.60	1.20	1.80	2.40	3.00	3.60	4.20	4.80	5.40	6.00
5 PIASTRES	1916-1939	7.00	833	5.80	0.19	.19	.38	.76	1.14	1.52	1.90	3.80	5.70	7.60	9.50	11.40	13.30	15.20	17.10	19.00
5 PIASTRES	1956-1960	3.50	720	2.50	0.08	.08	.16	.32	.48	.64	.80	1.60	2.40	3.20	4.00	4.80	5.60	6.40	7.20	8.00
5 PIASTRES	1964	2.50	720	1.80	0.06	.06	.12	.24	.36	.48	.60	1.20	1.80	2.40	3.00	3.60	4.20	4.80	5.40	6.00
10 PIASTRES	1916-1939	14.00	833	11.70	0.38	.38	.76	1.52	2.28	3.04	3.80	7.60	11.40	15.20	19.00	22.80	26.60	30.40	34.20	38.00

Coin Denomination	Years of Issue	Coin Wt. Grams	Purity	Silver Wt. Grams	Silver Troy Oz.	Silver Value—U.S. Dollars														
						$1	$2	$4	$6	$8	$10	$20	$30	$40	$50	$60	$70	$80	$90	$100
EGYPT - CONT'D.																				
10 PIASTRES	1955	7.00	625	4.40	0.14	.14	.28	.56	.84	1.12	1.40	2.80	4.20	5.60	7.00	8.40	9.80	11.20	12.60	14.00
10 PIASTRES	1956-1960	7.00	720	5.00	0.16	.16	.32	.64	.96	1.28	1.60	3.20	4.80	6.40	8.00	9.60	11.20	12.80	14.40	16.00
10 PIASTRES	1964	5.00	720	3.60	0.12	.12	.24	.48	.72	.96	1.20	2.40	3.60	4.80	6.00	7.20	8.40	9.60	10.80	12.00
20 PIASTRES	1916-1939	28.00	833	23.30	0.75	.75	1.50	3.00	4.50	6.00	7.50	15.00	22.50	30.00	37.50	45.00	52.50	60.00	67.50	75.00
20 PIASTRES	1956-1960	14.00	720	10.10	0.32	.32	.64	1.28	1.92	2.56	3.20	6.40	9.60	12.80	16.00	19.20	22.40	25.60	28.80	32.00
25 PIASTRES	1956-1960	17.50	720	12.60	0.41	.41	.82	1.64	2.46	3.28	4.10	8.20	12.30	16.40	20.50	24.60	28.70	32.80	36.90	41.00
25 PIASTRES	1964	10.00	720	7.20	0.23	.23	.46	.92	1.38	1.84	2.30	4.60	6.90	9.20	11.50	13.80	16.10	18.40	20.70	23.00
25 PIASTRES	1970-1973	6.30	720	4.50	0.14	.14	.28	.56	.84	1.12	1.40	2.80	4.20	5.60	7.00	8.40	9.80	11.20	12.60	14.00
50 PIASTRES	1956	28.00	900	25.20	0.81	.81	1.62	3.24	4.86	6.48	8.10	16.20	24.30	32.40	40.50	48.60	56.70	64.80	72.90	81.00
50 PIASTRES	1964	20.00	720	14.40	0.46	.46	.92	1.84	2.76	3.68	4.60	9.20	13.80	18.40	23.00	27.60	32.20	36.80	41.40	46.00
50 PIASTRES	1970	12.50	720	9.00	0.29	.29	.58	1.16	1.74	2.32	2.90	5.80	8.70	11.60	14.50	17.40	20.30	23.20	26.10	29.00
1 POUND	1968	25.00	833	20.80	0.67	.67	1.34	2.68	4.02	5.36	6.70	13.40	20.10	26.80	35.50	40.20	46.90	53.60	60.30	67.00
1 POUND	1970-1973	25.00	720	18.00	0.58	.58	1.16	2.32	3.48	4.64	5.80	11.60	17.40	23.20	29.00	34.80	40.60	46.40	52.20	58.00
1 POUND	1974-1978	15.00	720	10.80	0.35	.35	.70	1.40	2.10	2.80	3.50	7.00	10.50	14.00	17.50	21.00	24.50	28.00	31.50	35.00
EL SALVADOR																				
1 PESO	1971	2.30	999	2.30	0.07	.07	.14	.28	.42	.56	.70	1.40	2.10	2.80	3.50	4.20	4.90	5.60	6.30	7.00
5 COLONES	1971	11.50	999	11.50	0.37	.37	.74	1.48	2.22	2.96	3.70	7.40	11.10	14.80	18.50	22.20	25.90	29.60	33.30	37.00
EQUATORIAL GUIANA																				
25 PESETAS	1970	5.00	999	5.00	0.16	.16	.32	.64	.96	1.28	1.60	3.20	4.80	6.40	8.00	9.60	11.20	12.80	14.40	16.00
50 PESETAS	1970	10.00	999	10.00	0.32	.32	.64	1.28	1.92	2.56	3.20	6.40	9.60	12.80	16.00	19.20	22.40	25.60	28.80	32.00
75 PESETAS	1970	15.00	999	15.00	0.48	.48	.96	1.92	2.88	3.84	4.80	9.60	14.40	19.20	24.00	28.80	33.60	38.40	43.20	48.00
100 PESETAS	1970	20.00	999	20.00	0.64	.64	1.28	2.56	3.84	5.12	6.40	12.80	19.20	25.60	32.00	38.40	44.80	51.20	57.60	64.00
150 PESETAS	1970	30.00	999	30.00	0.96	.96	1.92	3.84	5.76	7.68	9.60	19.20	28.80	38.40	48.00	57.60	67.20	76.80	86.40	96.00
200 PESETAS	1970	40.00	999	40.00	1.29	1.29	2.58	5.16	7.74	10.32	12.90	25.80	38.70	51.60	64.50	77.40	90.30	103.20	116.10	129.00
1000 EKUELE	1978	21.40	925	19.80	0.64	.64	1.28	2.56	3.84	5.12	6.40	12.80	19.20	25.60	32.00	38.40	44.80	51.20	57.60	64.00
200 EKUELES	1978	42.90	925	39.70	1.28	1.28	2.56	5.12	7.68	10.24	12.80	25.60	38.40	51.20	64.00	76.80	89.60	102.40	115.20	128.00
ESTONIA																				
1 KROON	1933	6.00	500	3.00	0.96	.96	1.92	3.84	5.76	7.68	9.60	19.20	28.80	38.40	48.00	57.60	67.20	76.80	86.40	96.00
2 KROONI	1930-1932	12.00	500	6.00	1.93	1.93	3.86	7.72	11.58	15.44	19.30	38.60	57.90	77.20	96.50	115.80	135.10	154.40	173.70	193.00
ETHIOPIA																				
10 BIR	1979	28.30	925	26.20	0.84	.84	1.68	3.36	5.04	6.72	8.40	16.80	25.20	33.60	42.00	50.40	58.80	67.20	75.60	84.00

Coin Denomination	Years of Issue	Coin Wt. Grams	Purity	Silver Wt. Grams	Silver Troy Oz.	Silver Value—U.S. Dollars $1	$2	$4	$6	$8	$10	$20	$30	$40	$50	$60	$70	$80	$90	$100
ETHIOPIA - CONT'D.																				
25 BIR	1979	35.00	925	32.30	1.04	1.04	2.08	4.16	6.24	8.32	10.40	20.80	31.20	41.60	52.00	62.40	72.80	83.20	93.60	104.00
FALKLAND ISLANDS																				
50 PENCE	1977	28.30	925	26.20	0.84	.84	1.68	3.36	5.04	6.72	8.40	16.80	25.20	33.60	42.00	50.40	58.80	67.20	75.60	84.00
5 POUNDS	1979	28.30	925	26.20	0.84	.84	1.68	3.36	5.04	6.72	8.40	16.80	25.20	33.60	42.00	50.40	58.80	67.20	75.60	84.00
10 POUNDS	1979	35.00	925	32.40	1.04	1.04	2.08	4.16	6.24	8.32	10.40	20.80	31.20	41.60	52.00	62.40	72.80	83.20	93.60	104.00
FIJI ISLANDS																				
6 PENCE	1934-1941	2.80	500	1.40	0.04	.04	.08	.16	.24	.32	.40	.80	1.20	1.60	2.00	2.40	2.80	3.20	3.60	4.00
6 PENCE	1942-1943	2.80	900	2.50	0.08	.08	.16	.32	.48	.64	.80	1.60	2.40	3.20	4.00	4.80	5.60	6.40	7.20	8.00
1 SHILLING	1934-1941	5.70	500	2.80	0.09	.09	.18	.36	.54	.71	.90	1.80	2.70	3.60	4.50	5.40	6.30	7.20	8.10	9.00
1 SHILLING	1942-1943	5.70	900	5.10	0.16	.16	.32	.64	.96	1.28	1.60	3.20	4.80	6.40	8.00	9.60	11.20	12.80	14.40	16.00
1 FLORIN	1934-1941	11.30	500	5.70	0.18	.18	.36	.72	1.08	1.44	1.80	3.60	5.40	7.20	9.00	10.80	12.60	14.40	16.20	18.00
1 FLORIN	1942-1943	11.30	900	10.20	0.33	.33	.66	1.32	1.98	2.64	3.30	6.60	9.90	13.20	16.50	19.80	23.10	26.40	29.70	33.00
1 DOLLAR	1970-1976	27.30	925	25.20	0.81	.81	1.62	3.24	4.86	6.48	8.10	16.20	24.30	32.40	40.50	48.60	56.70	64.80	72.90	84.00
10 DOLLARS	1977-1978	28.30	925	26.20	0.84	.84	1.68	3.36	5.04	6.72	8.40	16.80	25.20	33.60	42.00	50.40	58.80	67.20	75.60	84.00
20 DOLLARS	1978	35.00	925	32.40	1.04	1.04	2.08	4.16	6.24	8.32	10.40	20.80	31.20	41.60	52.00	62.40	72.80	83.20	93.60	104.00
FINLAND																				
25 PENNIA	1865-1917	1.30	750	1.00	0.03	.03	.06	.12	.18	.24	.30	.60	.90	1.20	1.50	1.80	2.10	2.40	2.70	3.00
50 PENNIA	1864-1917	2.50	750	1.90	0.06	.06	.12	.24	.36	.48	.60	1.20	1.80	2.40	3.00	3.60	4.20	4.80	5.40	6.00
1 MARKKAA	1864-1915	5.20	868	4.50	0.14	.14	.28	.56	.84	1.12	1.40	2.80	4.20	5.60	7.00	8.40	9.80	11.20	12.60	14.00
1 MARKKAA	1964-1968	6.40	350	2.20	0.07	.07	.14	.28	.42	.56	.70	1.40	2.10	2.80	3.50	4.20	4.90	5.60	6.30	7.00
2 MARKKAA	1865-1908	10.40	868	9.00	0.29	.29	.58	1.16	1.74	2.32	2.90	5.80	8.70	11.60	14.50	17.40	20.30	23.20	26.10	29.00
10 MARKKAA	1967	24.00	900	21.60	0.69	.69	1.38	2.76	4.14	5.52	6.90	13.80	20.70	27.60	34.50	41.40	48.30	55.20	62.10	69.00
10 MARKKAA	1970	22.80	500	11.40	0.38	.38	.76	1.52	2.28	3.04	3.80	7.60	11.40	15.20	19.00	22.80	26.60	30.40	34.20	38.00
10 MARKKAA	1971	24.20	500	12.10	0.39	.39	.78	1.56	2.34	3.12	3.90	7.80	11.70	15.60	19.50	23.40	27.30	31.20	35.10	39.00
10 MARKKAA	1975	23.50	500	11.80	0.38	.38	.76	1.52	2.28	3.04	3.80	7.60	11.40	15.20	19.00	22.80	26.60	30.40	34.20	38.00
10 MARKKAA	1977	21.80	500	10.90	0.35	.35	.70	1.40	2.10	2.80	3.50	7.00	10.50	14.00	17.50	21.00	24.50	28.00	31.50	35.00
25 MARKKAA	1978	26.30	500	13.20	0.42	.42	.84	1.68	2.52	3.36	4.20	8.40	12.60	16.80	21.00	25.20	29.40	33.60	37.80	42.00
100 MARKKAA	1956-1960	5.20	500	2.60	0.08	.08	.16	.32	.48	.64	.80	1.60	2.40	3.20	4.00	4.80	5.60	6.40	7.20	8.00
200 MARKKAA	1956-1959	8.30	500	4.20	0.14	.14	.28	.56	.84	1.12	1.40	2.80	4.20	5.60	7.00	8.40	9.80	11.20	12.60	14.00
500 MARKKAA	1951-1952	12.00	500	6.00	0.19	.19	.38	.76	1.14	1.52	1.90	3.80	5.70	7.60	9.50	11.40	13.30	15.20	17.10	19.00
1000 MARKKAA	1960	14.00	875	12.30	0.40	.40	.80	1.60	2.40	3.20	4.00	8.00	12.00	16.00	20.00	24.00	28.00	32.00	36.00	40.00

Coin Denomination	Years of Issue	Coin Wt. Grams	Purity	Silver Wt. Grams	Silver Troy Oz.	Silver Value—U.S. Dollars														
						$1	$2	$4	$6	$8	$10	$20	$30	$40	$50	$60	$70	$80	$90	$100
FRANCE																				
20 CENTIMES	1849-1863	1.00	900	0.90	0.03	.03	.06	.12	.18	.24	.30	.60	.90	1.20	1.50	1.80	2.10	2.40	2.70	3.00
20 CENTIMES	1864-1869	1.00	835	0.83	0.03	.03	.06	.12	.18	.24	.30	.60	.90	1.20	1.50	1.80	2.10	2.40	2.70	3.00
25 CENTIMES	1845-1848	1.30	900	1.20	0.04	.04	.08	.16	.24	.32	.40	.80	1.20	1.60	2.00	2.40	2.80	3.20	3.60	4.00
50 CENTIMES	1845-1863	2.50	900	2.30	0.07	.07	.14	.28	.42	.56	.70	1.40	2.10	2.80	3.50	4.20	4.90	5.60	6.30	7.00
50 CENTIMES	1864-1920	2.50	835	2.10	0.07	.07	.14	.28	.42	.56	.70	1.40	2.10	2.80	3.50	4.20	4.90	5.60	6.30	7.00
1 FRANC	1849-1864	5.00	900	4.50	0.14	.14	.28	.56	.84	1.12	1.40	2.80	4.20	5.60	7.00	8.40	9.80	11.20	12.60	14.00
1 FRANC	1866-1920	5.00	835	4.20	0.14	.14	.28	.56	.84	1.12	1.40	2.80	4.20	5.60	7.00	8.40	9.80	11.20	12.60	14.00
2 FRANCS	1849-1859	10.00	900	9.00	0.29	.29	.58	1.16	1.74	2.32	2.90	5.80	8.70	11.60	14.50	17.40	20.30	23.20	26.10	29.00
2 FRANCS	1866-1920	10.00	835	8.40	0.27	.27	.54	1.08	1.62	2.16	2.70	5.40	8.10	10.80	13.50	16.20	18.90	21.60	24.30	27.00
5 FRANCS	1848-1878	25.00	900	22.50	0.72	.72	1.44	2.88	4.32	5.76	7.20	14.40	21.60	28.80	36.00	43.20	50.40	57.60	64.80	72.00
5 FRANCS	1960-1969	12.00	835	10.00	0.32	.32	.64	1.28	1.92	2.56	3.20	6.40	9.60	12.80	16.00	19.20	22.40	25.60	28.80	32.00
10 FRANCS	1929-1939	10.00	680	6.80	0.22	.22	.44	.88	1.32	1.76	2.20	4.40	6.60	8.80	11.00	13.20	15.40	17.60	19.80	22.00
10 FRANCS	1964-1973	25.00	900	22.50	0.72	.72	1.44	2.88	4.32	5.76	7.20	14.40	21.60	28.80	36.00	43.20	50.40	57.60	64.80	72.00
20 FRANCS	1929-1939	20.00	680	13.60	0.44	.44	.88	1.76	2.64	3.52	4.40	8.80	13.20	17.60	22.00	26.40	30.80	35.20	39.60	44.00
50 FRANCS	1974-1977	30.00	900	27.00	0.87	.87	1.74	3.48	5.22	6.96	8.70	17.40	26.10	34.80	43.50	52.20	60.90	69.60	78.30	87.00
FRENCH INDO-CHINA																				
10 CENTIMES	1885-18897	2.70	900	2.40	0.08	.08	.16	.32	.48	.64	.80	1.60	2.40	3.20	4.00	4.80	5.60	6.40	7.20	8.00
10 CENTIMES	1898-1919	2.70	835	2.30	0.07	.07	.14	.28	.42	.56	.70	1.40	2.10	2.80	3.50	4.20	4.90	5.60	6.30	7.00
10 CENTIMES	1921-1937	2.70	680	1.80	0.06	.06	.12	.24	.36	.48	.60	1.20	1.80	2.40	3.00	3.60	4.20	4.80	5.40	6.00
20 CENTIMES	1885-1909	5.40	900	4.90	0.16	.16	.32	.64	.96	1.28	1.60	3.20	4.80	6.40	8.00	9.60	11.20	12.80	14.40	16.00
20 CENTIMES	1890-1916	5.40	835	4.50	0.14	.14	.28	.56	.84	1.12	1.40	2.80	4.20	5.60	7.00	8.40	9.80	11.20	12.60	14.00
20 CENTIMES	1921-1937	5.40	680	3.70	0.12	.12	.24	.48	.72	.96	1.20	2.40	3.60	4.80	6.00	7.20	8.40	9.60	10.80	12.00
50 CENTIMES	1885-1936	3.60	900	12.20	0.39	.39	.78	1.56	2.34	3.12	3.90	7.80	11.70	15.60	19.50	23.40	27.30	31.20	35.10	39.00
1 PIASTRE	1885-1928	27.00	900	24.30	0.78	.78	1.56	3.12	4.68	6.24	7.80	15.60	23.40	31.20	39.00	46.80	54.60	62.40	70.20	78.00
1 PIASTRE	1931	20.00	900	18.00	0.58	.58	1.16	2.32	3.48	4.64	5.80	11.60	17.40	23.20	29.00	34.80	40.60	46.40	52.20	58.00
FURJAIRAH																				
1 RIYAL	1969-1970	3.00	1000	3.00	0.10	.10	.20	.40	.60	.80	1.00	2.00	3.00	4.00	5.00	6.00	7.00	8.00	9.00	10.00
2 RIYALS	1969-1970	6.00	1000	6.00	0.19	.19	.38	.76	1.14	1.52	1.90	3.80	5.70	7.60	9.50	11.40	13.30	15.20	17.10	19.00
5 RIYALS	1969-1970	15.00	1000	15.00	0.48	.48	.96	1.92	2.88	3.84	4.80	9.60	14.40	19.20	24.00	28.80	33.60	38.40	43.20	48.00
10 RIYALS	1969-1970	30.00	1000	30.00	0.96	.96	1.92	3.84	5.76	7.68	9.60	19.20	28.80	38.40	48.00	57.60	67.20	76.80	86.40	96.00
GAMBIA																				
8 SHILLINGS	1970	33.70	925	31.20	1.00	1.00	2.00	4.00	6.00	8.00	10.00	20.00	30.00	40.00	50.00	60.00	70.00	80.00	90.00	100.00
10 DALASIS	1975	28.30	500	14.10	0.45	.45	.90	1.80	2.70	3.60	4.50	9.00	13.50	18.00	22.50	27.00	31.50	36.00	40.50	45.00

Coin Denomination	Years of Issue	Coin Wt. Grams	Purity	Silver Wt. Grams	Silver Troy Oz.	Silver Value—U.S. Dollars $1	$2	$4	$6	$8	$10	$20	$30	$40	$50	$60	$70	$80	$90	$100
GAMBIA - CONT'D.																				
10 DALASIS	1975	28.30	925	26.20	0.84	.84	1.68	3.36	5.04	6.72	8.40	16.80	25.20	33.60	42.00	50.40	58.80	67.20	75.60	84.00
GERMANY																				
20 PFENNIG	1873-1877	1.10	900	0.90	0.03	.03	.06	.12	.18	.24	.30	.60	.90	1.20	1.50	1.80	2.10	2.40	2.70	3.00
50 PFENNIG	1875-1903	2.80	900	2.50	0.08	.08	.16	.32	.48	.64	.80	1.60	2.40	3.20	4.00	4.80	5.60	6.40	7.20	8.00
1/2 MARK	1905-1919	2.80	900	2.50	0.08	.08	.16	.32	.48	.64	.80	1.60	2.40	3.20	4.00	4.80	5.60	6.40	7.20	8.00
1 MARK	1873-1916	5.60	900	5.00	0.16	.16	.32	.64	.96	1.28	1.60	3.20	4.80	6.40	8.00	9.60	11.20	12.80	14.40	16.00
1 MARK	1924-1927	5.00	500	2.50	0.08	.08	.16	.32	.48	.64	.80	1.60	2.40	3.20	4.00	4.80	5.60	6.40	7.20	8.00
2 MARKS	1876-1914	11.10	900	10.00	0.32	.32	.64	1.28	1.92	2.56	3.20	6.40	9.60	12.80	16.00	19.20	22.40	25.60	28.80	32.00
2 MARKS	1925-1931	10.00	500	5.00	0.16	.16	.32	.64	.96	1.28	1.60	3.20	4.80	6.40	8.00	9.60	11.20	12.80	14.40	16.00
2 MARKS	1933-1936	8.00	625	5.00	0.16	.16	.32	.64	.96	1.28	1.60	3.20	4.80	6.40	8.00	9.60	11.20	12.80	14.40	16.00
3 MARKS	1908-1915	6.70	900	15.00	0.48	.48	.96	1.92	2.88	3.84	4.80	9.60	14.40	19.20	24.00	28.80	33.60	38.40	43.20	48.00
3 MARKS	1924-1932	15.00	500	7.50	0.24	.24	.48	.96	1.44	1.92	2.40	4.80	7.20	9.60	12.00	14.40	16.80	19.20	21.60	24.00
5 MARKS	1874-1914	27.80	900	25.00	0.80	.80	1.60	3.20	4.80	6.40	8.00	16.00	24.00	32.00	40.00	48.00	56.00	64.00	72.00	80.00
5 MARKS	1925-1932	25.00	500	12.50	0.40	.40	.80	1.60	2.40	3.20	4.00	8.00	12.00	16.00	20.00	24.00	28.00	32.00	36.00	40.00
5 MARKS	1933-1939	13.90	900	12.50	0.40	.40	.80	1.60	2.40	3.20	4.00	8.00	12.00	16.00	20.00	24.00	28.00	32.00	36.00	40.00
GERMANY, WEST																				
5 MARKS	1951-1978	11.20	625	7.00	0.23	.23	.46	.92	1.38	1.84	2.30	4.60	6.90	9.20	11.50	13.80	16.10	18.40	20.70	23.00
10 MARKS	1972	15.50	625	9.70	0.31	.31	.62	1.24	1.86	2.48	3.10	6.20	9.30	12.40	15.50	18.60	21.70	24.80	27.90	31.00
GERMANY, EAST																				
10 MARKS	1966-1967	17.00	800	13.60	0.44	.44	.88	1.76	2.64	3.52	4.40	8.80	13.20	17.60	22.00	26.40	30.80	35.20	39.60	44.00
10 MARKS	1968-1971, 1973	17.40	625	10.9	0.35	.35	.70	1.40	2.10	2.80	3.50	7.00	10.50	14.00	17.50	21.00	24.50	28.00	31.50	35.00
20 MARKS	1966-1967	29.90	800	23.90	0.77	.77	1.54	3.08	4.62	6.16	7.70	15.40	23.10	30.80	38.50	46.20	53.90	61.60	69.30	77.00
20 MARKS	1968-1971, 1973-1974	20.90	625	13.10	0.42	.42	.84	1.68	2.52	3.36	4.20	8.40	12.60	16.80	21.00	25.20	29.40	33.60	37.80	42.00
20 MARKS	1977-1979	20.90	500	10.50	0.34	.34	.68	1.36	2.04	2.72	3.40	6.80	10.20	13.60	17.00	20.40	23.80	27.20	30.60	34.00
GHANA																				
10 SHILLINGS	1958	28.30	925	26.20	0.84	.84	1.68	3.36	5.04	6.72	8.40	16.80	25.20	33.60	42.00	50.40	58.80	67.20	75.60	84.00

Coin Denomination	Years of Issue	Coin Wt. Grams	Purity	Silver Wt. Grams	Silver Troy Oz.	Silver Value—U.S. Dollars														
						$1	$2	$4	$6	$8	$10	$20	$30	$40	$50	$60	$70	$80	$90	$100
GIBRALTAR																				
1 CROWN	1967	28.30	500	14.20	0.46	.46	.92	1.84	2.76	3.68	4.60	9.20	13.80	18.40	23.00	27.60	32.20	36.80	41.40	46.00
25 PENCE	1971	28.30	500	14.20	0.46	.46	.92	1.84	2.76	3.68	4.60	9.20	13.80	18.40	23.00	27.60	32.20	36.80	41.40	46.00
25 NEW PENCE	1972	28.30	500	14.20	0.46	.46	.92	1.84	2.76	3.68	4.60	9.20	13.80	18.40	23.00	27.60	32.20	36.80	41.40	46.00
25 NEW PENCE	1972	28.30	925	26.20	0.84	.84	1.68	3.36	5.04	6.72	8.40	16.80	25.20	33.60	42.00	50.40	58.80	67.20	75.60	84.00
GREAT BRITAIN																				
3 PENCE	1834-1920	1.40	925	1.30	0.04	.04	.08	.16	.24	.32	.40	.80	1.20	1.60	2.00	2.40	2.80	3.20	3.60	4.00
3 PENCE	1920-1944	1.40	500	0.70	0.02	.02	.04	.08	.12	.16	.20	.40	.60	.80	1.00	1.20	1.40	1.60	1.80	2.00
6 PENCE	1838-1920	2.80	925	2.60	0.08	.08	.16	.32	.48	.64	.80	1.60	2.40	3.20	4.00	4.80	5.60	6.40	7.20	8.00
6 PENCE	1920-1946	2.80	500	1.40	0.05	.05	.10	.20	.30	.40	.50	1.00	1.50	2.00	2.50	3.00	3.50	4.00	4.50	5.00
1 SHILLING	1838-1919	5.70	925	5,29	0.17	.17	.34	.68	1.02	1.36	1.70	3.40	5.10	6.80	8.50	10.20	11.90	13.60	15.30	17.00
1 SHILLING	1920-1946	5.70	500	2.80	0.09	.09	.18	.36	.54	.72	.90	1.80	2.70	3.60	4.50	5.40	6.30	7.20	8.10	9.00
1 FLORIN	1851-1919	11.30	925	10.50	0.34	.34	.68	1.36	2.04	2.72	3.40	6.80	10.20	13.60	17.00	20.40	23.80	27.20	30.60	34.00
1 FLORIN	1920-1946	11.30	500	5.70	0.18	.18	.36	.72	1.08	1.44	1.80	3.60	5.40	7.20	9.00	10.80	12.60	14.40	16.20	18.00
1/2 CROWN	1839-1919	14.10	925	13.10	0.42	.42	.84	1.68	2.52	3.36	4.28	8.40	12.60	16.80	21.00	25.20	29.40	33.60	37.80	42.00
1/2 CROWN	1920-1946	14.10	500	7.10	0.23	.23	.46	.92	1.38	1.84	2.30	4.60	6.90	9.20	11.50	13.80	16.10	18.40	20.70	23.00
1 CROWN	1887-1902	28.30	925	26.20	0.84	.84	1.68	3.36	5.04	6.72	8.40	16.80	25.20	33.60	42.00	50.40	58.80	67.20	75.60	84.00
1 CROWN	1927-1937	28.80	500	14.10	0.45	.45	.90	1.80	2.70	3.60	4.50	9.00	13.50	18.00	22.50	27.00	31.50	36.00	40.50	45.00
1 TRADE DOLLAR	1895-1934	26.80	900	24.10	0.77	.77	1.54	3.08	4.62	6.16	7.70	15.40	23.10	30.80	38.50	46.20	53.90	61.60	69.30	77.00
25 NEW PENCE	1972	28.30	925	26.20	0.84	.84	1.68	3.36	5.04	6.72	8.40	16.80	25.20	33.60	42.00	50.40	58.80	67.20	75.60	84.00
25 NEW PENCE	1977	28.30	925	26.20	0.84	.84	1.68	3.36	5.04	6.72	8.40	16.80	25.20	33.60	42.00	50.40	58.80	67.20	75.60	84.00
GREECE																				
1 DRACHMA	1868-1911	5.00	835	4.20	0.14	.14	.28	.56	.84	1.12	1.40	2.80	4.20	5.60	7.00	8.40	9.80	11.20	12.60	14.00
2 DRACHMAI	1868-1911	10.00	835	8.40	0.27	.27	.54	1.08	1.62	2.16	2.70	5.40	8.10	10.80	13.50	16.20	18.90	21.60	24.30	27.00
5 DRACHMAI	1875-1876	25.00	900	22.50	0.72	.72	1.44	2.88	4.32	5.76	7.20	14.40	21.60	28.80	36.00	43.20	50.40	57.60	64.80	72.00
10 DRACHMAI	1930	7.00	500	3.50	0.11	.11	.22	.44	.66	.88	1.10	2.20	3.30	4.40	5.50	6.60	7.70	8.80	9.90	11.00
20 DRACHMAI	1930	11.30	500	5.70	0.18	.18	.36	.72	1.08	1.44	1.80	3.60	5.40	7.20	9.00	10.80	12.60	14.40	16.20	18.00
20 DRACHMAI	1960-1965	7.60	835	6.30	0.20	.20	.40	.80	1.20	1.60	2.00	4.00	6.00	8.00	10.00	12.00	14.00	16.00	18.00	20.00
30 DRACHMAI	1963	18.00	835	15.00	0.48	.48	.96	1.92	2.88	3.84	4.80	9.60	14.40	19.20	24.00	28.80	33.60	38.40	43.20	48.00
30 DRACHMAI	1964	12.00	835	10.00	0.32	.32	.64	1.28	1.92	2.56	3.20	6.40	9.60	12.80	16.00	19.20	22.40	25.60	28.80	32.00
50 DRACHMAI	1967	12.00	835	10.00	0.32	.32	.64	1.28	1.92	2.56	3.20	6.40	9.60	12.80	16.00	19.20	22.40	25.60	28.80	32.00
100 DRACHMAI	1967	25.00	835	20.90	0.67	.67	1.34	2.68	4.02	5.36	6.70	13.40	20.10	26.80	33.50	40.20	46.90	53.60	60.30	67.00
GUATEMALA																				
5 CENTAVOS	1925-1964	1.70	720	1.20	0.04	.04	.08	.16	.24	.32	.40	.80	1.20	1.60	2.00	2.40	2.80	3.20	3.60	4.00
10 CENTAVOS	1925-1964	3.40	720	2.40	0.08	.08	.16	.32	.48	.64	.80	1.60	2.40	3.20	4.00	4.80	5.60	6.40	7.20	8.00

Coin Denomination	Years of Issue	Coin Wt. Grams	Purity	Silver Wt. Grams	Silver Troy Oz.	Silver Value—U.S. Dollars														
						$1	$2	$4	$6	$8	$10	$20	$30	$40	$50	$60	$70	$80	$90	$100
GUATEMALA - CONT'D.																				
25 CENTAVOS	1881-1893	5.00	835	4.20	0.14	.14	.28	.56	.84	1.12	1.40	2.80	4.20	5.60	7.00	8.40	9.80	11.20	12.60	14.00
25 CENTAVOS	1943-1964	8.40	720	6.00	0.19	.19	.38	.76	1.14	1.52	1.90	3.80	5.70	7.60	9.50	11.40	13.30	15.20	17.10	19.00
50 CENTAVOS	1870	10.00	835	8.40	0.27	.27	.54	1.08	1.62	2.16	2.70	5.40	8.10	10.80	13.50	16.20	18.90	21.60	24.30	27.00
50 CENTAVOS	1962-1963	11.90	720	8.60	0.28	.28	.56	1.12	1.68	2.24	2.80	5.60	8.40	11.20	14.00	16.80	19.60	22.40	25.20	28.00
1 PESO	1866-1897	20.00	900	18.00	0.58	.58	1.16	2.32	3.48	4.64	5.80	11.60	17.40	23.20	29.00	34.80	40.60	46.40	52.20	58.00
GUINEA																				
100 FRANCS	1969-1970	5.80	1000	5.80	0.19	.19	.38	.76	1.14	1.52	1.90	3.80	5.70	7.60	9.50	11.40	13.30	15.20	17.10	19.00
200 FRANCS	1969-1970	11.60	1000	11.60	0.37	.37	.74	1.48	2.22	2.96	3.70	7.40	11.10	14.80	18.50	22.20	25.90	29.60	33.30	37.00
250 FRANCS	1969-1970	14.50	1000	14.50	0.47	.47	.94	1.88	2.82	3.76	4.70	9.40	14.10	18.80	23.50	28.20	32.90	37.60	42.30	47.00
500 FRANCS	1969-1970	28.90	1000	28.90	0.93	.93	1.86	3.72	5.58	7.44	9.30	18.60	27.90	37.20	46.50	55.80	65.10	74.40	83.70	93.00
500 SYLIS	1977	28.90	925	26.70	0.86	.86	1.72	3.44	5.16	6.88	8.60	17.20	25.80	34.40	43.00	51.60	60.20	68.80	77.40	86.00
GUINEA - BISSAU																				
10 ESCUDOS	1952	5.00	720	3.60	0.12	.12	.24	.48	.72	.96	1.20	2.40	3.60	4.80	6.00	7.20	8.40	9.60	10.80	12.00
20 ESCUDOS	1952	10.00	720	7.20	0.23	.23	.46	.92	1.38	1.84	2.30	4.60	6.90	9.20	11.50	13.80	16.10	18.40	20.70	23.00
HAITI																				
10 CENTIMES	1881-1894	2.50	835	2.10	0.07	.07	.14	.28	.42	.56	.70	1.40	2.10	2.80	3.50	4.20	4.90	5.60	6.30	7.00
20 CENTIMES	1881-1895	5.00	835	4.20	0.14	.14	.28	.56	.84	1.12	1.40	2.80	4.20	5.60	7.00	8.40	9.80	11.20	12.60	14.00
50 CENTIMES	1882-1895	12.50	835	10.40	0.33	.33	.66	1.32	1.98	2.64	3.30	6.60	9.90	13.20	16.50	19.80	23.10	26.40	29.70	33.00
5 GOURDES	1967-1971	23.50	1000	23.50	0.76	.76	1.52	3.04	4.56	6.08	7.60	15.20	22.80	30.40	38.00	45.60	53.20	60.80	68.40	76.00
10 GOURDES	1967-1971	47.20	1000	47.20	1.52	1.52	3.04	6.08	9.12	12.16	15.20	30.40	45.60	60.80	76.00	91.20	106.40	121.60	136.80	152.00
25 GOURDES	1967-1970	117.60	1000	117.60	3.78	3.78	7.56	15.12	22.68	30.24	37.80	75.60	113.40	151.20	189.00	226.80	264.80	302.40	340.20	378.00
25 GOURDES	1973-1975	8.40	925	7.80	0.25	.25	.50	1.00	1.50	2.00	2.50	5.00	7.50	10.00	12.50	15.00	17.50	20.00	22.50	25.00
25 GOURDES	1973	16.80	925	15.50	0.50	.50	1.00	2.00	3.00	4.00	5.00	10.00	15.00	20.00	25.00	30.00	35.00	40.00	45.00	50.00
50 GOURDES	1973-1977	21.50	925	19.90	0.64	.64	1.28	2.56	3.84	5.12	6.40	12.80	19.20	25.60	32.00	38.40	44.80	51.20	57.60	64.00
100 GOURDES	1977	43.00	925	39.80	1.28	1.28	2.56	5.12	7.68	10.24	12.80	25.60	38.40	51.20	64.00	76.80	89.60	102.40	115.20	128.00
HONDURAS																				
5 CENTAVOS	1883-1896	1.30	900	1.10	0.04	.04	.08	.16	.24	.32	.40	.80	1.20	1.60	2.00	2.40	2.80	3.20	3.60	4.00
10 CENTAVOS	1883-1900	2.50	900	2.30	0.07	.07	.14	.28	.42	.56	.70	1.40	2.10	2.80	3.50	4.20	4.90	5.60	6.30	7.00
20 CENTAVOS	1931-1958	2.50	900	2.30	0.07	.07	.14	.28	.42	.56	.70	1.40	2.10	2.80	3.50	4.20	4.90	5.60	6.30	7.00
25 CENTAVOS	1883-1896	6.30	900	5.60	0.08	.18	.36	.72	1.08	1.44	1.80	3.60	5.40	7.20	9.00	10.80	12.60	14.40	16.20	18.00

Coin Denomination	Years of Issue	Coin Wt. Grams	Purity	Silver Wt. Grams	Silver Troy Oz.	Silver Value—U.S. Dollars $1	$2	$4	$6	$8	$10	$20	$30	$40	$50	$60	$70	$80	$90	$100
HONDURAS - CONT'D.																				
25 CENTAVOS	1899-1913	6.30	835	5.20	0.17	.17	.34	.68	1.02	1.36	1.70	3.40	5.10	6.80	8.50	10.20	11.90	13.60	15.30	17.00
50 CENTAVOS	1883-1897	12.50	900	11.30	0.36	.36	.72	1.44	2.16	2.88	3.60	7.20	10.80	14.40	18.00	21.60	25.20	28.80	32.40	36.00
50 CENTAVOS	1931-1951	6.30	900	5.60	0.18	.18	.36	.72	1.08	1.44	1.80	3.60	5.40	7.20	9.00	10.80	12.60	14.40	16.20	18.00
1 PESO	1881-1914	25.00	900	22.30	0.72	.72	1.44	2.88	4.32	5.76	7.20	14.40	21.60	28.80	36.00	43.20	50.40	57.60	64.80	72.00
1 LEMPIRA	1931-1937	12.50	900	11.30	0.36	.36	.72	1.44	2.16	2.88	3.60	7.20	10.80	14.40	18.00	21.60	25.20	28.80	32.40	36.00
1 LEMPIRA	1971	6.30	900	5.60	0.18	.18	.36	.72	1.08	1.44	1.80	3.60	5.40	7.20	9.00	10.80	12.60	14.40	16.20	18.00
2 LEMPIRA	1971	12.50	900	11.30	0.36	.36	.72	1.44	2.16	2.88	3.60	7.20	10.80	14.40	18.00	21.60	25.20	28.80	32.40	36.00
5 LEMPIRA	1971	25.00	900	22.50	0.72	.72	1.44	2.88	4.32	5.76	7.20	14.40	21.60	28.80	36.00	43.20	50.40	57.60	64.80	72.00
HONG KONG																				
5 CENTS	1866-1933	1.40	800	1.10	0.04	.04	.08	.16	.24	.32	.40	.80	1.20	1.60	2.00	2.40	2.80	3.20	3.60	4.00
10 CENTS	1863-1905	2.70	800	2.20	0.07	.07	.14	.28	.42	.56	.70	1.40	2.10	2.80	3.50	4.20	4.90	5.60	6.30	7.00
20 CENTS	1863-1905	5.40	800	4.30	0.14	.14	.28	.56	.84	1.12	1.40	2.80	4.20	5.60	7.00	8.40	9.80	11.20	12.60	14.00
50 CENTS	1890-1905	13.60	800	10.90	0.35	.35	.70	1.40	2.10	2.80	3.50	7.00	10.50	14.00	17.50	21.00	24.50	28.00	31.50	35.00
HUNGARY																				
10 KRAJCZAR	1868-1888	2.00	400	0.80	0.03	.03	.06	.12	.18	.24	.30	.60	.90	1.20	1.50	1.80	2.10	2.40	2.70	3.00
20 KRAJCZAR	1868-1872	2.70	500	1.30	0.04	.04	.08	.16	.24	.32	.40	.80	1.20	1.60	2.00	2.40	2.80	3.20	3.60	4.00
1 FORINT	1868-1892	12.20	900	11.10	0.36	.36	.72	1.44	2.16	2.88	3.60	7.20	10.80	14.40	18.00	21.60	25.20	28.80	32.40	36.00
1 KORONA	1892-1916	5.00	835	4.20	0.14	.14	.28	.56	.84	1.12	1.40	2.80	4.20	5.60	7.00	8.40	9.80	11.20	12.60	14.00
2 KORONA	1912-1914	10.00	835	8.40	0.27	.27	.54	1.08	1.62	2.16	2.70	5.40	8.10	10.80	13.50	16.20	18.90	21.60	24.30	27.00
5 KORONA	1900-1909	24.00	900	21.60	0.69	.69	1.38	2.76	4.14	5.52	6.90	13.80	20.70	27.60	34.50	41.40	48.30	55.20	62.10	69.00
1 PENGO	1926-1939	5.00	640	3.20	0.10	.10	.20	.40	.60	.80	1.00	2.00	3.00	4.00	5.00	6.00	7.00	8.00	9.00	10.00
2 PENGO	1929-1939	10.00	640	6.40	0.21	.21	.42	.84	1.26	1.68	2.10	4.20	6.30	8.40	10.50	12.60	14.70	16.80	18.90	21.00
5 PENGO	1930-1939	25.00	640	16.00	0.51	.51	1.02	2.04	3.06	4.08	5.10	10.20	15.30	20.40	25.50	30.60	35.70	40.80	45.90	51.00
5 FORINT	1947-1948	12.00	500	6.00	0.19	.19	.38	.76	1.14	1.52	1.90	3.80	5.70	7.60	9.50	11.40	13.30	15.20	17.10	19.00
10 FORINT	1948	20.00	500	10.00	0.32	.32	.64	1.28	1.92	2.56	3.20	6.40	9.60	12.80	16.00	19.20	22.40	25.60	28.80	32.00
10 FORINT	1956	12.00	800	9.60	0.31	.31	.62	1.24	1.86	2.48	3.10	6.20	9.30	12.40	15.50	18.60	21.70	24.80	27.90	31.00
20 FORINT	1948	28.00	500	14.00	0.45	.45	.90	1.80	2.70	3.60	4.50	9.00	13.50	18.00	22.50	27.00	31.50	36.00	40.50	45.00
20 FORINT	1956	20.00	800	16.00	0.51	.51	1.02	2.04	3.06	4.08	5.10	10.20	15.30	20.40	25.50	30.60	35.70	40.80	45.90	51.00
25 FORINT	1956	25.00	800	20.00	0.64	.64	1.28	2.56	3.84	5.12	6.40	12.80	19.20	25.60	32.00	38.40	44.80	51.20	57.60	64.00
25 FORINT	1961-1967	17.50	750	13.10	0.42	.42	.84	1.68	2.52	3.36	4.20	8.40	12.60	16.80	21.00	25.20	29.40	33.60	37.80	42.00
25 FORINT	1966	12.00	640	7.70	0.25	.25	.50	1.00	1.50	2.00	2.50	5.00	7.50	10.00	12.50	15.00	17.50	20.00	22.50	25.00
50 FORINT	1961	20.00	835	16.70	0.54	.54	1.08	2.16	3.24	4.32	5.40	10.80	16.20	21.60	27.00	32.40	37.80	43.20	48.60	54.00
50 FORINT	1961	16.00	750	12.00	0.39	.39	.78	1.56	2.34	3.12	3.90	7.80	11.70	15.60	19.50	23.40	27.30	31.20	35.10	39.00
50 FORINT	1966-1974	16.00	640	10.20	0.33	.33	.66	1.32	1.98	2.64	3.30	6.60	9.90	13.20	16.50	19.80	23.10	26.40	29.70	33.00
100 FORINT	1967	28.00	750	21.00	0.68	.68	1.36	2.72	4.08	5.44	6.80	13.60	20.40	27.20	34.00	40.80	47.60	54.40	61.20	68.00
100 FORINT	1968	28.00	640	17.90	0.58	.58	1.16	2.32	3.48	4.64	5.80	11.60	17.40	23.20	29.00	34.80	40.60	46.40	52.20	58.00
100 FORINT	1969-1974	22.00	640	14.10	0.45	.45	.90	1.80	2.70	3.60	4.50	9.00	13.50	18.00	22.50	27.00	31.50	36.00	40.50	45.00
200 FORINT	1975-1978	28.00	640	17.90	0.58	.58	1.16	2.32	3.48	4.64	5.80	11.60	17.40	23.20	29.00	34.80	40.60	46.40	52.20	58.00

Coin Denomination	Years of Issue	Coin Wt. Grams	Purity	Silver Wt. Grams	Silver Troy Oz.	Silver Value—U.S. Dollars $1	$2	$4	$6	$8	$10	$20	$30	$40	$50	$60	$70	$80	$90	$100
ICELAND																				
500 KRONUR	1974	20.00	925	18.50	0.59	.59	1.18	2.36	3.54	4.72	5.90	11.80	17.70	23.60	29.50	35.40	41.30	47.20	53.10	59.00
100 KRONUR	1974	30.00	925	27.80	0.89	.89	1.78	3.56	5.34	7.12	8.90	17.80	26.70	35.60	44.50	53.40	62.30	71.20	80.10	89.00
INDIA																				
2 ANNAS	1862-1917	1.50	917	1.30	0.04	.04	.08	.16	.24	.32	.40	.80	1.20	1.60	2.00	2.40	2.80	3.20	3.60	4.00
1/4 RUPEE	1862-1936	2.90	917	2.70	0.09	.09	.18	.36	.54	.72	.90	1.80	2.70	3.60	4.50	5.40	6.30	7.20	8.10	9.00
1/4 RUPEE	1940-1945	2.90	500	1.50	0.05	.05	.10	.20	.30	.40	.50	1.00	1.50	2.00	2.50	3.00	3.50	4.00	4.50	5.00
1/2 RUPEE	1862-1936	5.80	917	5.30	0.17	.17	.34	.68	1.02	1.36	1.70	3.40	5.10	6.80	8.50	10.20	11.90	13.60	15.30	17.00
1/2 RUPEE	1941-1945	5.80	500	2.90	0.09	.09	.18	.36	.54	.72	.90	1.80	2.70	3.60	4.50	5.40	6.30	7.20	8.10	9.00
1 RUPEE	1862-1939	11.70	917	10.70	0.34	.34	.68	1.36	2.04	2.72	3.40	6.80	10.20	13.60	17.00	20.40	23.80	27.20	30.60	34.00
1 RUPEE	1939-1945	11.70	500	5.80	0.19	.19	.38	.76	1.14	1.52	1.90	3.80	5.70	7.60	9.50	11.40	13.30	15.20	17.10	19.00
10 RUPEES	1969-1971	15.00	800	12.00	0.39	.39	.78	1.56	2.34	3.12	3.90	7.80	11.70	15.60	19.50	23.40	27.30	31.20	35.10	39.00
10 RUPEES	1972-1977	22.30	500	11.20	0.36	.36	.72	1.44	2.16	2.88	3.60	7.20	10.80	14.40	18.00	21.60	25.20	28.80	32.40	36.00
10 RUPEES	1972	22.30	925	20.60	0.66	.66	1.32	2.64	3.96	5.28	6.60	13.20	19.80	26.40	33.00	39.60	46.20	52.80	59.40	66.00
20 RUPEES	1973	30.00	500	15.00	0.48	.48	.96	1.92	2.88	3.84	4.80	9.60	14.40	19.20	24.00	28.80	33.60	38.40	43.20	48.00
50 RUPEES	1974-1979	35.00	500	17.50	0.56	.56	1.12	2.24	3.36	4.48	5.60	11.20	16.80	22.40	28.00	33.60	39.20	44.80	50.40	56.00
INDONESIA																				
200 RUPIAH	1970	8.00	1000	8.00	0.26	.26	.52	1.04	1.56	2.08	2.60	5.20	7.80	10.40	13.00	15.60	18.20	20.80	23.40	26.00
250 RUPIAH	1970	10.00	1000	10.00	0.32	.32	.64	1.28	1.92	2.56	3.20	6.40	9.60	12.80	16.00	19.20	22.40	25.60	28.80	32.00
500 RUPIAH	1970	20.00	1000	20.00	0.64	.64	1.28	2.56	3.84	5.12	6.40	12.80	19.20	25.60	32.00	38.40	44.80	51.20	57.60	64.00
750 RUPIAH	1970	30.00	1000	30.00	0.96	.96	1.92	3.84	5.76	7.68	9.60	19.20	28.80	38.40	48.00	57.60	67.20	76.80	86.40	96.00
1000 RUPIAH	1970	40.00	1000	40.00	1.29	1.29	2.58	5.16	7.74	10.32	12.90	25.80	38.70	51.60	64.50	77.40	90.30	103.20	116.10	129.00
2000 RUPIAH	1974	28.30	500	14.10	0.45	.45	.90	1.80	2.70	3.60	4.50	9.00	13.50	18.00	22.50	27.00	31.50	36.00	40.50	45.00
2000 RUPIAH	1974	28.30	925	26.20	0.84	.84	1.68	3.36	5.04	6.72	8.40	16.80	25.20	33.60	42.00	50.40	58.80	67.20	75.60	84.00
5000 RUPIAH	1974	31.70	500	15.80	0.51	.51	1.02	2.04	3.06	4.08	5.10	10.20	15.30	20.40	25.50	30.60	35.70	40.80	45.90	51.00
5000 RUPIAH	1974	31.70	925	29.30	0.94	.94	1.88	3.76	5.64	7.52	9.40	18.80	28.20	37.60	47.00	56.40	65.80	75.20	84.60	94.00
IRAN																				
3 SHAHIS	1297-1342	0.80	900	0.70	0.02	.02	.04	.08	.12	.16	.20	.40	.60	.80	1.00	1.20	1.40	1.60	1.80	2.00
5 SHAHIS	1296-1343	1.30	900	1.10	0.04	.04	.08	.16	.24	.32	.40	.80	1.20	1.60	2.00	2.40	2.80	3.20	3.60	4.00
10 SHAHIS	1296-1343	2.50	900	2.30	0.07	.07	.14	.28	.42	.56	.70	1.40	2.10	2.80	3.50	4.20	4.90	5.60	6.30	7.00
10 SHAHIS	1296-1344	4.60	900	4.10	0.13	.13	.26	.52	.78	1.04	1.30	2.60	3.90	5.20	6.50	7.80	9.10	10.40	11.70	13.00
2 KRANS	1296-1344	9.20	900	8.30	0.27	.27	.54	1.08	1.62	2.16	2.70	5.40	8.10	10.80	13.50	16.20	18.90	21.60	24.30	27.00
5 KRANS	1296-1344	23.00	900	20.70	0.67	.67	1.34	2.68	4.02	5.36	6.70	13.40	20.10	26.80	33.50	40.20	46.90	53.60	60.30	67.00

Coin Denomination	Years of Issue	Coin Wt. Grams	Purity	Silver Wt. Grams	Silver Troy Oz.	Silver Value—U.S. Dollars $1	$2	$4	$6	$8	$10	$20	$30	$40	$50	$60	$70	$80	$90	$100
IRAN - CONT'D.																				
1/2 RIAL	1310-1315	2.50	830	2.10	0.07	.07	.14	.28	.42	.56	.70	1.40	2.10	2.80	3.50	4.20	4.90	5.60	6.30	7.00
1 RIAL	1310-1313	5.00	830	4.20	0.14	.14	.28	.56	.84	1.12	1.40	2.80	4.20	5.60	7.00	8.40	9.80	11.20	12.60	14.00
1 RIAL	1322-1330	1.60	600	1.00	0.03	.03	.06	.12	.18	.24	.30	.60	.90	1.20	1.50	1.80	2.10	2.40	2.70	3.00
2 RIALS	1310-1313	10.00	830	8.30	0.27	.27	.54	1.08	1.62	2.16	2.70	5.40	8.10	10.80	13.50	16.20	18.90	21.60	24.30	27.00
2 RIALS	1322-1330	3.20	600	1.90	0.06	.06	.12	.24	.36	.48	.60	1.20	1.80	2.40	3.00	3.60	4.20	4.80	5.40	6.00
5 RIALS	1310-1313	25.00	830	20.70	0.67	.67	1.34	2.68	4.02	5.36	6.70	13.40	20.10	26.80	33.50	40.20	46.90	53.60	60.30	67.00
5 RIALS	1322-1329	8.00	600	4.80	0.15	.15	.30	.60	.90	1.20	1.50	3.00	4.50	6.00	7.50	9.00	10.50	12.00	13.50	15.00
10 RIALS	1323-1326	16.00	600	9.60	0.31	.31	.62	1.24	1.86	2.48	3.10	6.20	9.30	12.40	15.50	18.60	21.70	24.80	27.90	31.00
25 RIALS	1971	7.50	999	7.50	0.24	.24	.48	.96	1.44	1.92	2.40	4.80	7.20	9.60	12.00	14.40	16.80	19.20	21.60	24.00
50 RIALS	1971	15.00	999	15.00	0.48	.48	.96	1.92	2.88	3.84	4.80	9.60	14.40	19.20	24.00	28.80	33.60	38.40	43.20	48.00
75 RIALS	1971	22.50	999	22.50	0.72	.72	1.44	2.88	4.32	5.76	7.20	14.40	21.60	28.80	36.00	43.20	50.40	57.60	64.80	72.00
100 RIALS	1971	30.00	999	30.00	0.96	.96	1.92	3.84	5.76	7.68	9.60	19.20	28.80	38.40	48.00	57.60	67.20	76.80	86.40	96.00
200 RIALS	1971	60.00	999	60.00	1.93	1.93	3.86	7.72	11.58	15.44	19.30	38.60	57.90	77.20	96.50	115.80	135.10	154.40	173.70	193.00
DATES INCLUDE AH AND SH DATES.																				
IRAQ																				
20 FILS	1349-1375	3.60	500	1.80	0.06	.06	.12	.24	.36	.48	.60	1.20	1.80	2.40	3.00	3.60	4.20	4.80	5.40	6.00
25 FILS	1379	2.50	500	1.30	0.04	.04	.08	.16	.24	.32	.40	.80	1.20	1.60	2.00	2.40	2.80	3.20	3.60	4.00
50 FILS	1349-1352	9.00	500	4.50	0.14	.14	.28	.56	.84	1.12	1.40	2.80	4.20	5.60	7.00	8.40	9.80	11.20	12.60	14.00
50 FILS	1378	5.00	500	2.50	0.08	.08	.16	.32	.48	.64	.80	1.60	2.40	3.20	4.00	4.80	5.60	6.40	7.20	8.00
100 FILS	1375-1379	10.00	500	5.00	0.16	.16	.32	.64	.96	1.28	1.60	3.20	4.80	6.40	8.00	9.60	11.20	12.80	14.40	16.00
200 FILS	1350	20.00	500	10.00	0.32	.32	.64	1.28	1.92	2.56	3.20	6.40	9.60	12.80	16.00	19.20	22.40	25.60	28.80	32.00
500 FILS	1379	37.50	500	18.80	0.60	.60	1.20	2.40	3.60	4.80	6.00	12.00	18.00	24.00	30.00	36.00	42.00	48.00	54.00	60.00
500 FILS	1393	20.00	500	10.00	0.32	.32	.64	1.28	1.92	2.56	3.20	6.40	9.60	12.80	16.00	19.20	22.40	25.60	28.80	32.00
1 DINAR	1390-1397	31.00	900	27.90	0.90	.90	1.80	3.60	5.40	7.20	9.00	18.00	27.00	36.00	45.00	54.00	63.00	72.00	81.00	90.00
DATES INCLUDE AH DATES.																				
IRELAND																				
1 SHILLING	1928-1942	5.70	750	4.20	0.14	.14	.28	.56	.84	1.12	1.40	2.80	4.20	5.60	7.00	8.40	9.80	11.20	12.60	14.00
1 FLORIN	1928-1943	11.30	750	8.50	0.27	.27	.54	1.08	1.62	2.16	2.70	5.40	8.10	10.80	13.50	16.20	18.90	21.60	24.30	27.00
1/2 CROWN	1928-1943	14.10	750	10.60	0.34	.34	.68	1.36	2.04	2.72	3.40	6.80	10.20	13.60	17.00	20.40	23.80	27.20	30.60	34.00
10 SHILLINGS	1966	18.10	833	15.10	0.49	.49	.98	1.96	2.94	3.92	4.90	9.80	14.70	19.60	24.50	29.40	34.30	39.20	44.10	49.00
ISLE OF MAN																				
1/2 PENNY	1975-1978	2.10	925	1.90	0.06	.06	.12	.24	.36	.48	.60	1.20	1.80	2.40	3.00	3.60	4.20	4.80	5.40	6.00
1 PENNY	1975-1978	4.20	925	3.90	0.13	.13	.26	.52	.78	1.04	1.30	2.60	3.90	5.20	6.50	7.80	9.10	10.40	11.70	13.00

Coin Denomination	Years of Issue	Coin Wt. Grams	Purity	Silver Wt. Grams	Silver Troy Oz.	Silver Value—U.S. Dollars $1	$2	$4	$6	$8	$10	$20	$30	$40	$50	$60	$70	$80	$90	$100
ISLE OF MAN - CONT'D.																				
2 PENCE	1975-1978	8.40	925	7.80	0.25	.25	.50	1.00	1.50	2.00	2.50	5.00	7.50	10.00	12.50	15.00	17.50	20.00	22.50	25.00
5 PENCE	1975-1978	6.50	925	6.00	0.19	.19	.38	.76	1.14	1.52	1.90	3.80	5.70	7.60	9.50	11.40	13.30	15.20	17.10	19.00
10 PENCE	1975-1978	13.00	925	12.00	0.39	.39	.78	1.56	2.34	3.12	3.90	7.80	11.70	15.60	19.50	23.40	27.30	31.20	35.10	39.00
25 PENCE	1972-1978	28.30	925	26.20	0.84	.84	1.68	3.36	5.04	6.72	8.40	16.80	25.20	33.60	42.00	50.40	58.80	67.20	75.60	84.00
50 PENCE	1975-1978	15.50	925	14.30	0.46	.46	.92	1.84	2.76	3.68	4.60	9.20	13.80	18.40	23.00	27.60	32.20	36.80	41.40	46.00
1 CROWN	1970-1979	28.30	925	26.20	0.84	.84	1.68	3.36	5.04	6.72	8.40	16.80	25.20	33.60	42.00	50.40	58.80	67.20	75.60	84.00
ISRAEL																				
250 PRUTOT	1949	14.40	500	7.20	0.23	.23	.46	.92	1.38	1.84	2.30	4.60	6.90	9.20	11.50	13.80	16.10	18.40	20.70	23.00
500 PRUTOT	1949	25.50	500	12.80	0.41	.41	.82	1.64	2.46	3.28	4.10	8.20	12.30	16.40	20.50	24.60	28.70	32.80	36.90	41.00
5 LIROT	1958-1967	25.00	900	22.50	0.72	.72	1.44	2.88	4.32	5.76	7.20	14.40	21.60	28.80	36.00	43.20	50.40	57.60	64.80	72.00
5 LIROT	1972	20.00	750	15.00	0.48	.48	.96	1.92	2.88	3.84	4.80	9.60	14.40	19.20	24.00	28.80	33.60	38.40	43.20	48.00
5 LIROT	1973	20.00	500	10.00	0.32	.32	.64	1.28	1.92	2.56	3.20	6.40	9.60	12.80	16.00	19.20	22.40	25.60	28.80	32.00
10 LIROT	1967-1976	26.00	900	23.40	0.75	.75	1.50	3.00	4.50	6.00	7.50	15.00	22.50	30.00	37.50	45.00	52.50	60.00	67.50	75.00
10 LIROT	1974-1975	20.00	500	10.00	0.32	.32	.64	1.28	1.92	2.56	3.20	6.40	9.60	12.80	16.00	19.20	22.40	25.60	28.80	32.00
25 LIROT	1974	26.00	935	24.30	0.78	.78	1.56	3.12	4.68	6.24	7.80	15.60	23.40	31.20	39.00	46.80	54.60	62.40	70.20	78.00
25 LIROT	1975-1976	26.00	900	23.40	0.75	.75	1.50	3.00	4.50	6.00	7.50	15.00	22.50	30.00	37.50	45.00	52.50	60.00	67.50	75.00
25 LIROT	1975-1976	30.00	800	24.00	0.77	.77	1.54	3.08	4.62	6.16	7.70	15.40	23.10	30.80	38.50	46.20	53.90	61.60	69.30	77.00
25 LIROT	1977	20.00	500	10.00	0.32	.32	.64	1.28	1.92	2.56	3.20	6.40	9.60	12.80	16.00	19.20	22.40	25.60	28.80	32.00
25 LIROT	1977	20.00	900	18.00	0.58	.58	1.16	2.32	3.48	4.64	5.80	11.60	17.40	23.20	29.00	34.80	40.60	46.40	52.20	58.00
50 LIROT	1978-1979	20.00	500	10.00	0.32	.32	.64	1.28	1.92	2.56	3.20	6.40	9.60	12.80	16.00	19.20	22.40	25.60	28.80	32.00
100 LIROT	1979	20.00	500	10.00	0.32	.32	.64	1.28	1.92	2.56	3.20	6.40	9.60	12.80	16.00	19.20	22.40	25.60	28.80	32.00
ITALY																				
20 CENTESIMI	1863-1867	1.00	835	0.80	0.03	.03	.06	.12	.18	.24	.30	.60	.90	1.20	1.50	1.80	2.10	2.40	2.70	3.00
50 CENTESIMI	1866-1867	2.50	835	2.10	0.07	.07	.14	.28	.42	.56	.70	1.40	2.10	2.80	3.50	4.20	4.90	5.60	6.30	7.00
1 LIRA	1863-1917	5.00	835	4.20	0.14	.14	.28	.56	.84	1.12	1.40	2.80	4.20	5.60	7.00	8.40	9.80	11.20	12.60	14.00
2 LIRE	1863-1917	10.00	835	8.40	0.27	.27	.54	1.08	1.62	2.16	2.70	5.40	8.10	10.80	13.50	16.20	18.90	21.60	24.30	27.00
5 LIRE	1861-1878	25.00	900	22.50	0.72	.72	1.44	2.88	4.32	5.76	7.20	14.40	21.60	28.80	36.00	43.20	50.40	57.60	64.80	72.00
5 LIRE	1926-1941	5.00	835	4.20	0.14	.14	.28	.56	.84	1.12	1.40	2.80	4.20	5.60	7.00	8.40	9.80	11.20	12.60	14.00
10 LIRE	1926-1936	10.00	835	8.40	0.27	.27	.54	1.08	1.62	2.16	2.70	5.40	8.10	10.80	13.50	16.20	18.90	21.60	24.30	27.00
20 LIRE	1927-1941	15.00	800	12.00	0.39	.39	.78	1.56	2.34	3.12	3.90	7.80	11.70	15.60	19.50	23.40	27.30	31.20	35.10	39.00
500 LIRE	1958-1976	11.00	835	9.20	0.30	.30	.60	1.20	1.80	2.40	3.00	6.00	9.00	12.00	15.00	18.00	21.00	24.00	27.00	30.00
1000 LIRE	1970	14.00	835	11.70	0.38	.38	.76	1.52	2.28	3.04	3.80	7.60	11.40	15.20	19.00	22.80	26.60	30.40	34.20	38.00

Coin Denomination	Years of Issue	Coin Wt. Grams	Purity	Silver Wt. Grams	Silver Troy Oz.	Silver Value—U.S. Dollars $1	$2	$4	$6	$8	$10	$20	$30	$40	$50	$60	$70	$80	$90	$100
JAMAICA																				
5 DOLLARS	1971-1973	42.20	925	39.00	1.25	1.25	2.50	5.00	7.50	10.00	12.50	25.00	37.50	50.00	62.50	75.00	87.50	100.00	112.50	125.00
5 DOLLARS	1974-1979	42.20	500	21.10	0.68	.68	1.36	2.72	4.08	5.44	6.80	13.60	20.40	27.20	34.00	40.80	47.60	54.40	61.20	68.00
10 DOLLARS	1972-1979	48.60	925	45.00	1.45	1.45	2.90	5.80	8.70	11.60	14.50	29.00	43.50	58.00	72.50	87.00	101.50	116.00	130.50	145.00
25 DOLLARS	1978-1979	136.10	925	125.90	4.05	4.05	8.10	16.20	24.30	32.40	40.50	81.00	121.50	162.00	202.50	243.00	283.50	324.00	364.50	405.00
JAPAN																				
5 SEN	1870-1880	1.30	800	1.10	0.04	.04	.08	.16	.24	.32	.40	.80	1.20	1.60	2.00	2.40	2.80	3.20	3.60	4.00
10 SEN	1870-1912	2.70	800	2.20	0.07	.07	.14	.28	.42	.56	.70	1.40	2.10	2.80	3.50	4.20	4.90	5.60	6.30	7.00
10 SEN	1912-1917	2.30	720	1.60	0.05	.05	.10	.20	.30	.40	.50	1.00	1.50	2.00	2.50	3.00	3.50	4.00	4.50	5.00
20 SEN	1870-1905	5.40	800	4.30	0.14	.14	.28	.56	.84	1.12	1.40	2.80	4.20	5.60	7.00	8.40	9.80	11.20	12.60	14.00
20 SEN	1906-1911	4.10	800	3.20	0.10	.10	.20	.40	.60	.80	1.00	2.00	3.00	4.00	5.00	6.00	7.00	8.00	9.00	10.00
50 SEN	1870-1905	12.50	800	10.00	0.32	.32	.64	1.28	1.92	2.56	3.20	6.40	9.60	12.80	16.00	19.20	22.40	25.60	28.80	32.00
50 SEN	1906-1917	10.30	800	8.20	0.26	.26	.52	1.04	1.56	2.08	2.60	5.20	7.80	10.40	13.00	15.60	18.20	20.80	23.40	26.00
50 SEN	1922-1938	5.00	720	3.60	0.12	.12	.24	.48	.72	.96	1.20	2.40	3.60	4.80	6.00	7.20	8.40	9.60	10.80	12.00
1 YEN	1874-1914	27.00	900	24.30	0.78	.78	1.56	3.12	4.68	6.24	7.80	15.60	23.40	31.20	39.00	46.80	54.60	62.40	70.20	78.00
100 YEN	1957-1966	4.80	600	2.90	0.09	.09	.18	.36	.54	.72	.90	1.80	2.70	3.60	4.50	5.40	6.30	7.20	8.10	9.00
1000 YEN	1964	20.00	925	18.50	0.59	.59	1.18	2.36	3.54	4.72	5.90	11.80	17.70	23.60	29.50	35.40	41.30	47.20	53.10	59.00
JERSEY																				
50 PENCE	1972	5.40	925	5.00	0.16	.16	.32	.64	.96	1.28	1.60	3.20	4.80	6.40	8.00	9.60	11.20	12.80	14.40	16.00
1 POUND	1972	10.80	925	10.00	0.32	.32	.64	1.28	1.92	2.56	3.20	6.40	9.60	12.80	16.00	19.20	22.40	25.60	28.80	32.00
2 POUNDS	1972	21.60	925	20.00	0.64	.64	1.28	2.56	3.84	5.12	6.40	12.80	19.20	25.60	32.00	38.40	44.80	51.20	57.60	64.00
2-1/2 POUNDS	1972	27.10	925	25.10	0.81	.81	1.62	3.24	4.86	6.48	8.10	16.20	24.30	32.40	40.50	48.60	56.70	64.80	72.90	81.00
JORDAN																				
1/2 DINAR	1969	20.00	1000	20.00	0.64	.64	1.28	2.56	3.84	5.12	6.40	12.80	19.20	25.60	32.00	38.40	44.80	51.20	57.60	64.00
3/4 DINAR	1969	30.00	1000	30.00	0.96	.96	1.92	3.84	5.76	7.68	9.60	19.20	28.80	38.40	48.00	57.60	67.20	76.80	86.40	96.00
1 DINAR	1969	40.00	1000	40.00	1.29	1.29	2.58	5.16	7.74	10.32	12.90	25.80	38.70	51.60	64.50	77.40	90.30	103.20	116.10	129.00
2-1/2 DINARS	1977	28.30	925	26.20	0.84	.84	1.68	3.36	5.04	6.72	8.40	16.80	25.20	33.60	42.00	50.40	58.80	67.20	75.60	84.00
3 DINARS	1977	35.00	925	32.40	1.04	1.04	2.08	4.16	6.24	8.32	10.40	20.80	31.20	41.60	52.00	62.40	72.80	83.20	93.60	104.00
KOREA																				
50 WON	1970	2.80	1000	2.80	0.09	.09	.18	.36	.54	.72	.90	1.80	2.70	3.60	4.50	5.40	6.30	7.20	8.10	9.00
100 WON	1970	5.60	1000	5.60	0.18	.18	.36	.72	1.08	1.44	1.80	3.60	5.40	7.20	9.00	10.80	12.60	14.40	16.20	18.00

Coin Denomination	Years of Issue	Coin Wt. Grams	Purity	Silver Wt. Grams	Silver Troy Oz.	$1	$2	$4	$6	$8	$10	$20	$30	$40	$50	$60	$70	$80	$90	$100
KOREA - CONT'D.																				
200 WON	1970	11.20	1000	11.20	0.36	.36	.72	1.44	2.16	2.88	3.60	7.20	10.80	14.40	18.00	21.60	25.20	28.80	32.40	36.00
250 WON	1970	14.00	1000	14.00	0.45	.45	.90	1.80	2.70	3.60	4.50	9.00	13.50	18.00	22.50	27.00	31.50	36.00	40.50	45.00
500 WON	1970	28.00	1000	28.00	0.90	.90	1.80	3.60	5.40	7.20	9.00	18.00	27.00	36.00	45.00	54.00	63.00	72.00	81.00	90.00
1000 WON	1970	56.00	1000	56.00	1.80	1.80	3.60	7.20	10.80	14.40	18.00	36.00	54.00	72.00	90.00	108.00	126.00	144.00	162.00	180.00
KUWAIT																				
2 DINARS	1976	28.30	500	14.10	0.45	.45	.90	1.80	2.70	3.60	4.50	9.00	13.50	18.00	22.50	27.00	31.50	36.00	40.50	45.00
LAOS																				
1000 KIP	1971	2.40	925	2.20	0.07	.07	.14	.28	.42	.56	.70	1.40	2.10	2.80	3.50	4.20	4.90	5.60	6.30	7.00
2500 KIP	1971	5.90	925	5.50	0.18	.18	.36	.72	1.08	1.44	1.80	3.60	5.40	7.20	9.00	10.80	12.60	14.40	16.20	18.00
5000 KIP	1971-1975	11.80	925	10.90	0.35	.35	.70	1.40	2.10	2.80	3.50	7.00	10.50	14.00	17.50	21.00	24.50	28.00	31.50	35.00
10,000 KIP	1971-1975	23.60	925	21.80	0.70	.70	1.40	2.80	4.20	5.60	7.00	14.00	21.00	28.00	35.00	42.00	49.00	56.00	63.00	70.00
LATVIA																				
1 LATS	1924	5.00	835	4.20	0.14	.14	.28	.56	.84	1.12	1.40	2.80	4.20	5.60	7.00	8.40	9.80	11.20	12.60	14.00
2 LATI	1925-1926	10.00	835	8.40	0.27	.27	.54	1.08	1.62	2.16	2.70	5.40	8.10	10.80	13.50	16.20	18.90	21.60	24.30	27.00
5 LATI	1929-1932	25.00	835	20.90	0.67	.67	1.34	2.68	4.02	5.36	6.70	13.40	20.10	26.80	33.50	40.20	46.90	53.60	60.30	67.00
LEBANON																				
10 PIASTRES	1929	2.00	680	1.40	0.05	.05	.10	.20	.30	.40	.50	1.00	1.50	2.00	2.50	3.00	3.50	4.00	4.50	5.00
25 PIASTRES	1929-1936	5.00	680	3.40	0.11	.11	.22	.44	.66	.88	1.10	2.20	3.30	4.40	5.50	6.60	7.70	8.80	9.90	11.00
50 PIASTRES	1929-1936	10.00	680	6.80	0.22	.22	.44	.88	1.32	1.76	2.20	4.40	6.60	8.80	11.00	13.20	15.40	17.60	19.80	22.00
LESOTHE																				
5 LICENTE	1966	2.80	900	2.50	0.08	.08	.16	.32	.48	.64	.80	1.60	2.40	3.20	4.00	4.80	5.60	6.40	7.20	8.00
10 LICENTE	1966	5.70	900	5.10	0.16	.16	.32	.64	.96	1.28	1.60	3.20	4.80	6.40	8.00	9.60	11.20	12.80	14.40	16.00
20 LICENTE	1966	11.30	900	10.20	0.33	.33	.66	1.32	1.98	2.64	3.30	6.60	9.90	13.20	16.50	19.80	23.10	26.40	29.70	33.00
50 LICENTE	1966	28.30	900	25.50	0.82	.82	1.64	3.28	4.92	6.56	8.20	16.40	24.60	32.80	41.00	49.20	57.40	65.60	73.80	82.00
10 MILOTI	1976	25.10	925	23.20	0.75	.75	1.50	3.00	4.50	6.00	7.50	15.00	22.50	30.00	37.50	45.00	52.50	60.00	67.50	75.00

Column group $1–$100: Silver Value—U.S. Dollars

Coin Denomination	Years of Issue	Coin Wt. Grams	Purity	Silver Wt. Grams	Silver Troy Oz.	Silver Value—U.S. Dollars $1	$2	$4	$6	$8	$10	$20	$30	$40	$50	$60	$70	$80	$90	$100
LIBERIA																				
10 CENTS	1896-1961	2.10	900	1.90	0.06	.06	.12	.24	.36	.48	.60	1.20	1.80	2.40	3.00	3.60	4.20	4.80	5.40	6.00
25 CENTS	1896-1961	5.20	900	4.70	0.15	.15	.30	.60	.90	1.20	1.50	3.00	4.50	6.00	7.50	9.00	10.50	12.00	13.50	15.00
50 CENTS	1896-1961	11.00	900	9.90	0.32	.32	.64	1.28	1.92	2.56	3.20	6.40	9.60	12.80	16.00	19.20	22.40	25.60	28.80	32.00
1 DOLLAR	1961-1962	20.70	900	18.70	0.60	.60	1.20	2.40	3.60	4.80	6.00	12.00	18.00	24.00	30.00	36.00	42.00	48.00	54.00	60.00
5 DOLLARS	1973-1978	34.10	900	30.70	0.99	.99	1.98	3.96	5.94	7.92	9.90	19.80	29.70	39.60	49.50	59.40	69.30	79.20	89.10	99.00
LICHTENSTEIN																				
1 KRONE	1900-1915	5.00	835	4.20	0.14	.14	.28	.56	.84	1.12	1.40	2.80	4.20	5.60	7.00	8.40	9.80	11.20	12.60	14.00
2 KRONEN	1912=1915	10.00	835	8.40	0.27	.27	.54	1.08	1.62	2.16	2.70	5.40	8.10	10.80	13.50	16.20	18.90	21.60	24.30	27.00
5 KRONEN	1900-1915	24.00	900	21.60	0.69	.69	1.38	2.76	4.14	5.52	6.90	13.80	20.70	27.60	34.50	41.40	48.30	55.20	62.10	69.00
LITHUANIA																				
1 LITAS	1925	2.70	500	1.40	0.05	.05	.10	.20	.30	.40	.50	1.00	1.50	2.00	2.50	3.00	3.50	4.00	4.50	5.00
2 LITU	1925	5.40	500	2.70	0.09	.09	.18	.36	.54	.72	.90	1.80	2.70	3.60	4.50	5.40	6.30	7.20	8.10	9.00
5 LITAI	1925	13.50	500	6.80	0.22	.22	.44	.88	1.32	1.76	2.20	4.40	6.60	8.80	11.00	13.20	15.40	17.60	19.80	22.00
5 LITAI	1936	9.00	750	6.80	0.22	.22	.44	.88	1.32	1.76	2.20	4.40	6.60	8.80	11.00	13.20	15.40	17.60	19.80	22.00
10 LITU	1936-1938	18.00	750	13.50	0.43	.43	.86	1.72	2.58	3.44	4.30	8.60	12.90	17.20	21.50	25.80	30.10	34.40	38.70	43.00
LUXEMBOURG																				
5 FRANCS	1929	8.00	625	5.00	0.16	.16	.32	.64	.96	1.28	1.60	3.20	4.80	6.40	8.00	9.60	11.20	12.80	14.40	16.00
10 FRANCS	1929	13.10	750	9.80	0.32	.32	.64	1.28	1.92	2.56	3.20	6.40	9.60	12.80	16.00	19.20	22.40	25.60	28.80	32.00
20 FRANCS	1946	5.00	835	4.20	0.14	.14	.28	.56	.84	1.12	1.40	2.80	4.20	5.60	7.00	8.40	9.80	11.20	12.60	14.00
50 FRANCS	1946	12.50	835	10.40	0.33	.33	.66	1.32	1.98	2.64	3.30	6.60	9.90	13.20	16.50	19.80	23.10	26.40	29.70	33.00
100 FRANCS	1946	25.00	835	20.90	0.67	.67	1.34	2.68	4.02	5.36	6.70	13.40	20.10	26.80	33.50	40.20	46.90	53.60	60.30	67.00
100 FRANCS	1963-1964	18.00	835	15.00	0.48	.48	.96	1.92	2.88	3.84	4.80	9.60	14.40	19.20	24.00	28.80	33.60	38.40	43.20	48.00
250 FRANCS	1963	25.00	900	22.50	0.72	.72	1.44	2.88	4.32	5.76	7.20	14.40	21.60	28.80	36.00	43.20	50.40	57.60	64.80	72.00
MACAO																				
1 PATACA	1952	2.50	720	1.80	0.06	.06	.12	.24	.36	.48	.60	1.20	1.80	2.40	3.00	3.60	4.20	4.80	5.40	6.00
5 PATACAS	1952	15.00	720	10.80	0.35	.35	.70	1.40	2.10	2.80	3.50	7.00	10.50	14.00	17.50	21.00	24.50	28.00	31.50	35.00
5 PATACAS	1971	9.90	650	6.40	0.21	.21	.42	.84	1.26	1.68	2.10	4.20	6.30	8.40	10.50	12.60	14.70	16.80	18.90	21.00
20 PATACAS	1974	18.00	650	11.70	0.38	.38	.76	1.52	2.28	3.04	3.80	7.60	11.40	15.20	19.00	22.80	26.60	30.40	34.20	38.00
100 PATACAS	1978	28.30	925	26.20	0.84	.84	1.68	3.36	5.04	6.72	8.40	16.80	25.20	33.60	42.00	50.40	58.80	67.20	75.60	84.00

Coin Denomination	Years of Issue	Coin Wt. Grams	Purity	Silver Wt. Grams	Silver Troy Oz.	Silver Value—U.S. Dollars $1	$2	$4	$6	$8	$10	$20	$30	$40	$50	$60	$70	$80	$90	$100
MALAGASY																				
10 ARIARY	1978	9.00	925	8.30	0.27	.27	.54	1.08	1.62	2.16	2.70	5.40	8.10	10.80	13.50	16.20	18.90	21.60	24.30	27.00
20 ARIARY	1978	12.00	925	11.10	0.36	.36	.72	1.44	2.16	2.88	3.60	7.20	10.80	14.40	18.00	21.60	25.20	28.80	32.40	36.00
MALAWI																				
5 KWACHA	1978	28.30	925	26.20	0.84	.84	1.68	3.36	5.04	6.72	8.40	16.80	25.20	33.60	42.00	50.40	58.80	67.20	75.60	84.00
10 KWACHA	1974-1978	35.00	925	32.40	1.04	1.04	2.08	4.16	6.24	8.32	10.40	20.80	31.20	41.60	52.00	62.40	72.80	83.20	93.60	104.00
MALAYSIA																				
5 CENTS	1871-1903, 1910	1.40	800	1.10	0.04	.04	.08	.16	.24	.32	.40	.80	1.20	1.60	2.00	2.40	2.80	3.20	3.60	4.00
5 CENTS	1926-1935	1.40	600	0.80	0.03	.03	.06	.12	.18	.24	.30	.60	.90	1.20	1.50	1.80	2.10	2.40	2.70	3.00
5 CENTS	1918-1920	1.40	400	0.50	0.02	.02	.04	.08	.12	.16	.20	.40	.60	.80	1.00	1.20	1.40	1.60	1.80	2.00
10 CENTS	1871-1903, 1909-1917	2.70	800	2.20	0.07	.07	.14	.28	.42	.56	.70	1.40	2.10	2.80	3.50	4.20	4.90	5.60	6.30	7.00
10 CENTS	1926-1927	2.70	600	1.60	0.05	.05	.10	.20	.30	.40	.50	1.00	1.50	2.00	2.50	3.00	3.50	4.00	4.50	5.00
10 CENTS	1918-1920	2.70	400	1.10	0.04	.04	.08	.16	.24	.32	.40	.80	1.20	1.60	2.00	2.40	2.80	3.20	3.60	4.00
20 CENTS	1871-1903, 1910-1917	5.40	800	4.30	0.14	.14	.28	.56	.84	1.12	1.40	2.80	4.20	5.60	7.00	8.40	9.80	11.20	12.60	14.00
20 CENTS	1926-1935	5.40	600	3.30	0.11	.11	.22	.44	.66	.88	1.10	2.20	3.30	4.40	5.50	6.60	7.70	8.80	9.90	11.00
20 CENTS	1919	5.40	400	2.20	0.07	.07	.14	.28	.42	.56	.70	1.40	2.10	2.80	3.50	4.20	4.90	5.60	6.30	7.00
50 CENTS	1886-1905	10.10	800	6.10	0.20	.20	.40	.80	1.20	1.60	2.00	4.00	6.00	8.00	10.00	12.00	14.00	16.00	18.00	20.00
50 CENTS	1907-1908	10.10	900	9.10	0.29	.29	.58	1.16	1.74	2.32	2.90	5.80	8.70	11.60	14.50	17.40	18L90	23.20	26.10	29.00
50 CENTS	1920-1921	8.40	500	4.20	0.14	.14	.28	.56	.84	1.12	1.40	2.80	4.20	5.60	7.00	8.40	9.80	11.20	12.60	14.00
1 DOLLAR	1903-1904	27.00	900	24.30	0.78	.78	1.56	3.12	4.68	6.24	7.80	15.60	23.40	31.20	39.00	46.80	54.60	62.40	70.20	78.00
1 DOLLAR	1907-1909	20.20	900	18.20	0.59	.59	1.18	2.36	3.54	4.72	5.90	11.80	17.70	23.60	29.50	35.40	41.30	47.20	53.10	59.00
1 DOLLAR	1919-1926	16.90	500	8.40	0.27	.27	.54	1.08	1.62	2.16	2.70	5.40	8.10	10.80	13.50	16.20	18.90	21.60	24.30	27.00
1 RINGIT	1969,1979	17.00	925	15.70	0.50	.50	1.00	2.00	3.00	4.00	5.00	10.00	15.00	20.00	25.00	30.00	35.00	40.00	45.00	50.00
10 RINGIT	1976	10.90	917	10.00	0.32	.32	.64	1.28	1.92	2.56	3.20	6.40	9.60	12.80	16.00	19.20	22.40	25.60	28.80	32.00
15 RINGIT	1976	28.30	925	26.20	0.84	.84	1.68	3.36	5.04	6.72	8.40	16.80	25.20	33.60	42.00	50.40	58.80	67.20	75.60	84.00
25 RINGIT	1976-1977	35.00	925	32.40	1.04	1.04	2.08	4.16	6.24	8.32	10.40	20.80	31.20	41.60	52.00	62.40	72.80	83.20	93.60	104.00
MALAYA																				
5 CENTS	1939-1941	1.40	750	1.00	0.03	.03	.06	.12	.18	.24	.30	.60	.90	1.20	1.50	1.80	2.10	2.40	2.70	3.00
5 CENTS	1943-1945	1.40	500	0.70	0.02	.02	.04	.08	.12	.16	.20	.40	.60	.80	1.00	1.20	1.40	1.60	1.80	2.00
10 CENTS	1939-1941	2.70	750	2.00	0.06	.06	.12	.24	.36	.48	.60	1.20	1.80	2.40	3.00	3.60	4.20	4.80	5.40	6.00
10 CENTS	1943-1945	2.70	500	1.40	0.05	.05	.10	.20	.30	.40	.50	1.00	1.50	2.00	2.50	3.00	3.50	4.00	4.50	5.00

Coin Denomination	Years of Issue	Coin Wt. Grams	Purity	Silver Wt. Grams	Silver Troy Oz.	Silver Value—U.S. Dollars														
						$1	$2	$4	$6	$8	$10	$20	$30	$40	$50	$60	$70	$80	$90	$100
MALAYA - CONT'D.																				
20 CENTS	1939	5.40	750	4.10	0.13	.13	.26	.52	.78	1.04	1.30	2.60	3.90	5.20	6.50	7.80	9.10	10.40	11.70	13.00
20 CENTS	1943-1945	5.40	500	2.70	0.09	.09	.18	.36	.54	.72	.90	1.80	2.70	3.60	4.50	5.40	6.30	7.20	8.10	9.00
MALDIVE ISLANDS																				
20 RUFIYAA	1977	24.50	500	14.20	0.46	.46	.92	1.84	2.76	3.68	4.60	9.20	13.80	18.40	23.00	27.60	32.20	36.80	41.40	46.00
25 RUFIYAA	1978	28.20	500	14.10	0.46	.46	.92	1.84	2.76	3.68	4.60	9.20	13.80	18.40	23.00	27.60	32.20	36.80	41.40	46.00
MALI																				
10 FRANCS	1960	25.00	900	22.50	0.72	.72	1.44	2.88	4.32	5.76	7.20	14.40	21.60	28.80	36.00	43.20	50.40	57.60	64.80	72.00
MALTA																				
1 POUND	1972-1973	10.00	987	9.90	0.32	.32	.64	1.28	1.92	2.56	3.20	6.40	9.60	12.80	16.00	19.20	22.40	25.60	28.80	32.00
1 POUND	1977	5.70	925	5.20	0.17	.17	.34	.68	1.02	1.36	1.70	3.40	5.10	6.80	8.50	10.20	11.90	13.60	15.30	17.00
2 POUNDS	1972-1973	20.00	987	19.70	0.63	.63	1.26	2.52	3.78	5.04	6.30	12.60	18.90	25.20	31.50	37.80	44.10	50.40	56.70	63.00
2 POUNDS	1974-1976	10.00	987	9.90	0.32	.32	.64	1.28	1.92	2.56	3.20	6.40	9.60	12.80	16.00	19.20	22.40	25.60	28.80	32.00
2 POUNDS	1977	11.30	925	10.50	0.34	.34	.68	1.36	2.04	2.72	3.40	6.80	10.20	13.60	17.00	20.40	23.80	27.20	30.60	34.00
4 POUNDS	1974-1976	20.00	987	19.70	0.64	.64	1.28	2.56	3.84	5.12	6.40	12.80	19.20	25.60	32.00	38.40	44.80	51.20	57.60	64.00
5 POUNDS	1977	28.30	925	26.20	0.84	.84	1.68	3.36	5.04	6.72	8.40	16.80	25.20	33.60	42.00	50.40	58.80	67.20	75.60	84.00
MALTA {SOVEREIGN MILITARY ORDER}																				
9 TARI	1967-1978	9.00	900	8.10	0.26	.26	.52	1.04	1.56	2.08	2.60	5.20	7.80	10.40	13.00	15.60	18.20	20.80	23.40	26.00
1 SCUDO	1961-1978	12.00	986	11.80	0.38	.38	.76	1.52	2.28	3.04	3.80	7.60	11.40	15.20	19.00	22.80	26.60	30.40	34.20	38.00
2 SCUDI	1961-1978	24.00	986	26.70	0.86	.86	1.72	3.44	5.16	6.88	8.60	17.20	25.80	34.40	43.00	51.60	60.20	68.80	77.40	86.00
3 SCUDI	1968	12.00	800	9.60	0.31	.31	.62	1.24	1.86	2.48	3.10	6.20	9.30	12.40	15.50	18.60	21.70	24.80	27.90	31.00
MAURITIUS																				
10 CENTS	1877-1897	1.40	800	1.10	0.04	.04	.08	.16	.24	.32	.40	.80	1.20	1.60	2.00	2.40	2.80	3.20	3.60	4.00
20 CENTS	1877-1899	2.80	800	2.30	0.07	.07	.14	.28	.42	.56	.70	1.40	2.10	2.80	3.50	4.20	4.90	5.60	6.30	7.00

Coin Denomination	Years of Issue	Coin Wt. Grams	Purity	Silver Wt. Grams	Silver Troy Oz.	Silver Value—U.S. Dollars														
						$1	$2	$4	$6	$8	$10	$20	$30	$40	$50	$60	$70	$80	$90	$100
MAURITIUS - CONT'D.																				
1/4 RUPEE	1934-1938	2.80	916	2.60	0.08	.08	.16	.32	.48	.64	.80	1.60	2.40	3.20	4.00	4.80	5.60	6.40	7.20	8.00
1/4 RUPEE	1946	2.80	500	1.40	0.05	.05	.10	.20	.30	.40	.50	1.00	1.50	2.00	2.50	3.00	3.50	4.00	4.50	5.00
1/2 RUPEE	1934	5.70	916	5.20	0.17	.17	.34	.68	1.02	1.36	1.70	3.40	5.10	6.80	8.50	10.20	11.90	13.60	15.30	17.00
1/2 RUPEE	1946	5.70	500	2.80	0.09	.09	.18	.36	.54	.72	.90	1.80	2.70	3.60	4.50	5.40	6.30	7.20	8.10	9.00
1 RUPEE	1934-1938	11.30	916	10.40	0.33	.33	.66	1.32	1.98	2.64	3.30	6.60	9.90	13.20	16.50	19.80	23.10	26.40	29.70	33.00
25 RUPEES	1975-1978	25.30	500	12.70	0.41	.41	.82	1.64	2.46	3.28	4.10	8.20	12.30	16.40	20.50	24.60	28.70	32.80	36.90	41.00
25 RUPEES	1975-1978	28.30	925	26.20	0.84	.84	1.68	3.36	5.04	6.72	8.40	16.80	25.20	33.60	42.00	50.40	58.80	67.20	75.60	84.00
50 RUPEES	1975	31.70	500	15.80	0.51	.51	1.02	2.04	3.06	4.08	5.10	10.20	15.30	20.40	25.50	30.60	35.70	40.80	45.90	51.00
50 RUPEES	1975	31.50	925	32.40	1.04	1.04	2.08	4.16	6.24	8.32	10.40	20.80	31.20	41.60	52.00	62.40	72.80	83.20	93.60	104.00
MEXICO																				
1/2 REAL	1825-1869	1.70	903	1.50	0.05	.05	.10	.20	.30	.40	.50	1.00	1.50	2.00	2.50	3.00	3.50	4.00	4.50	5.00
1 REAL	1825-1869	3.40	903	3.10	0.10	.10	.20	.40	.60	.80	1.00	2.00	3.00	4.00	5.00	6.00	7.00	8.00	9.00	10.00
2 REALES	1825-1870	6.80	903	6.10	0.20	.20	.40	.80	1.20	1.60	2.00	4.00	6.00	8.00	10.00	12.00	14.00	16.00	18.00	20.00
4 REALES	1825-1870	13.50	903	12.20	0.39	.39	.78	1.56	2.34	3.12	3.90	7.80	11.70	15.60	19.50	23.40	27.30	31.20	35.10	39.00
8 REALES	1825-1897	27.10	903	24.40	0.78	.78	1.56	3.12	4.68	6.24	7.80	15.60	23.40	31.20	39.00	46.80	54.60	62.40	70.20	78.00
5 CENTAVOS	1868-1905	1.40	903	1.20	0.04	.04	.08	.16	.24	.32	.40	.80	1.20	1.60	2.00	2.40	2.80	3.20	3.60	4.00
10 CENTAVOS	1868-1905	2.70	903	2.40	0.08	.08	.16	.32	.48	.64	.80	1.60	2.40	3.20	4.00	4.80	5.60	6.40	7.20	8.00
10 CENTAVOS	1905-1914	2.50	800	2.00	0.06	.06	.12	.24	.36	.48	.60	1.20	1.80	2.40	3.00	3.60	4.20	4.80	5.40	6.00
10 CENTAVOS	1919	2.10	800	1.70	0.05	.05	.10	.20	.30	.40	.50	1.00	1.50	2.00	2.50	3.00	3.50	4.00	4.50	5.00
10 CENTAVOS	1925-1935	1.70	720	1.20	0.04	.04	.08	.16	.24	.32	.40	.80	1.20	1.60	2.00	2.40	2.80	3.20	3.60	4.00
20 CENTAVOS	1898-1905	5.40	903	4.90	0.16	.16	.32	.64	.96	1.28	1.60	3.20	4.80	6.40	8.00	9.60	11.20	12.80	14.40	16.00
20 CENTAVOS	1905-1914	5.00	800	4.00	0.13	.13	.26	.52	.78	1.04	1.30	2.60	3.90	5.20	6.50	7.80	9.10	10.40	11.70	13.00
20 CENTAVOS	1919	4.40	800	3.50	0.11	.11	.22	.44	.66	.88	1.10	2.20	3.30	4.40	5.50	6.60	7.70	8.80	9.90	11.00
20 CENTAVOS	1920-1943	3.30	720	2.40	0.08	.08	.16	.32	.48	.64	.80	1.60	2.40	3.20	4.00	4.80	5.60	6.40	7.20	8.00
25 CENTAVOS	1869-1892	6.80	903	6.10	0.20	.20	.40	.80	1.20	1.60	2.00	4.00	6.00	8.00	10.00	12.00	14.00	16.00	18.00	20.00
25 CENTAVOS	1950-1953	3.30	300	1.00	0.03	.03	.06	.12	.18	.24	.30	.60	.90	1.20	1.50	1.80	2.10	2.40	2.70	3.00
50 CENTAVOS	1875-1914	13.50	903	12.20	0.39	.39	.78	1.56	2.34	3.12	3.90	7.80	11.70	15.60	19.50	23.40	27.30	31.20	35.10	39.00
50 CENTAVOS	1905-1918	12.50	800	10.00	0.32	.32	.64	1.28	1.92	2.56	3.20	6.40	9.60	12.80	16.00	19.20	22.40	25.60	28.80	32.00
50 CENTAVOS	1918-1945	8.30	720	6.00	0.19	.19	.38	.76	1.14	1.52	1.90	3.80	5.70	7.60	9.50	11.40	13.30	15.20	17.10	19.00
50 CENTAVOS	1950-1951	6.70	300	2.00	0.06	.06	.12	.24	.36	.48	.60	1.20	1.80	2.40	3.00	3.60	4.20	4.80	5.40	6.00
1 PESO	1872-1914	27.10	903	24.40	0.78	.78	1.56	3.12	4.68	6.24	7.80	15.60	23.40	31.20	39.00	46.80	54.60	62.40	70.20	78.00
1 PESO	1918-1919	18.10	800	14.50	0.47	.47	.94	1.88	2.82	3.76	4.70	9.40	14.10	18.80	23.50	28.20	32.90	37.60	42.30	47.00
1 PESO	1920-1945	16.70	720	12.00	0.39	.39	.78	1.56	2.34	3.12	3.90	7.80	11.70	15.60	19.50	23.40	27.30	31.20	35.10	39.00
1 PESO	1947-1949	14.00	500	7.00	0.23	.23	.46	.92	1.38	1.84	2.30	4.60	6.90	9.20	11.50	13.80	16.10	18.40	20.70	23.00
1 PESO	1950	13.30	300	4.00	0.13	.13	.26	.52	.78	1.04	1.30	2.60	3.90	5.20	6.50	7.80	9.10	10.40	11.70	13.00
1 PESO	1957-1967	16.00	100	1.60	0.05	.05	.10	.20	.30	.40	.50	1.00	1.50	2.00	2.50	3.00	3.50	4.00	4.50	5.00
2 PESOS	1921	30.00	900	27.00	0.87	.87	1.74	3.48	5.22	6.96	8.70	17.40	26.10	34.80	43.50	52.20	60.90	69.60	78.30	87.00
5 PESOS	1947-1948	30.00	900	27.00	0.87	.87	1.74	3.48	5.22	6.96	8.70	17.40	26.10	34.80	43.50	52.20	60.90	69.60	78.30	87.00
5 PESOS	1951-1954	27.80	720	20.00	0.64	.64	1.28	2.56	3.84	5.12	6.40	12.80	19.20	25.60	32.00	38.40	44.80	51.20	57.60	64.00
5 PESOS	1955-1959	18.10	720	13.00	0.42	.42	.84	1.68	2.52	3.36	4.20	8.40	12.60	16.80	21.00	25.20	29.40	33.60	37.80	42.00

Coin Denomination	Years of Issue	Coin Wt. Grams	Purity	Silver Wt. Grams	Silver Troy Oz.	Silver Value—U.S. Dollars														
						$1	$2	$4	$6	$8	$10	$20	$30	$40	$50	$60	$70	$80	$90	$100
MEXICO - CONT'D.																				
10 PESOS	1955-1960	28.90	900	26.00	0.84	.84	1.68	3.36	5.04	6.72	8.40	16.80	25.20	33.60	42.00	50.40	58.80	67.20	75.60	84.00
25 PESOS	1968-1972	22.50	720	16.20	0.52	.52	1.04	2.08	3.12	4.16	5.20	10.40	15.60	20.80	26.00	31.20	36.40	41.60	46.80	52.00
100 PESOS	1977-1979	27.80	720	20.00	0.64	.64	1.28	2.56	3.84	5.12	6.40	12.80	19.20	25.60	32.00	38.40	44.80	51.20	57.60	64.00
1 TROY OUNCE	1949 1978-1979	33.60	925	31.10	1.00	1.00	2.00	4.00	6.00	8.00	10.00	20.00	30.00	40.00	50.00	60.00	70.00	80.00	90.00	100.00
MONACO																				
5 FRANCS	1960-1966	12.00	835	10.00	0.32	.32	.64	1.28	1.92	2.56	3.20	6.40	9.60	12.80	16.00	19.20	22.40	25.60	28.80	32.00
10 FRANCS	1966	25.00	900	22.50	0.72	.72	1.44	2.88	4.32	5.76	7.20	14.40	21.60	28.80	36.00	43.20	50.40	57.60	64.80	72.00
50 FRANCS	1974	30.00	900	27.00	0.87	.87	1.74	3.48	5.22	6.96	8.70	17.40	26.10	34.80	43.50	52.20	60.90	69.60	78.30	87.00
100 FRANCS	1974	36.00	999	36.00	1.16	1.16	2.32	4.64	6.96	9.28	11.60	23.20	34.80	46.40	58.00	69.60	81.20	92.80	104.40	116.00
MONGOLIA																				
10 MONGO	1925	1.80	500	0.90	0.03	.03	.06	.12	.18	.24	.30	.60	.90	1.20	1.50	1.80	2.10	2.40	2.70	3.00
15 MONGO	1925	2.70	500	1.40	0.05	.05	.10	.20	.30	.40	.50	1.00	1.50	2.00	2.50	3.00	3.50	4.00	4.50	5.00
20 MONGO	1925	3.60	500	1.80	0.06	.06	.12	.24	.36	.48	.60	1.20	1.80	2.40	3.00	3.60	4.20	4.80	5.40	6.00
50 MONGO	1925	10.00	900	9.00	0.29	.29	.58	1.16	1.74	2.32	2.90	5.80	8.70	11.60	14.50	17.40	18.90	23.20	26.10	29.00
1 TUKHRIK	1925	20.00	900	18.00	0.58	.58	1.16	2.32	3.48	4.64	5.80	11.60	17.40	23.20	29.00	34.80	40.60	46.40	52.20	58.00
10 TIKHRIK	1976	23.30	925	21.50	0.69	.69	1.38	2.76	4.14	5.52	6.90	13.80	20.70	27.60	34.50	41.40	48.30	55.20	62.10	69.00
25 TIKHRIK	1976	31.00	925	26.70	0.86	.86	1.72	3.44	5.16	6.88	8.60	17.20	25.80	34.40	43.00	51.60	60.20	68.80	77.40	86.00
MOROCCO																				
1/2 DIRHAM	1299-1321	1.30	835	1.00	0.03	.03	.06	.12	.18	.24	.30	.60	.90	1.20	1.50	1.80	2.10	2.40	2.70	3.00
1 DIRHAM	1299-1331	2.40	835	2.00	0.06	.06	.12	.24	.36	.48	.60	1.20	1.80	2.40	3.00	3.60	4.20	4.80	5.40	6.00
2-1/2 DIRHAM	1299-1331	6.20	835	5.20	0.17	.17	.34	.68	1.02	1.36	1.70	3.40	5.10	6.80	8.50	10.20	11.90	13.60	15.30	17.00
5 DIRHAMS	1299-1336	12.50	835	10.40	0.33	.33	.66	1.32	1.98	2.64	3.30	6.60	9.90	13.20	16.50	19.80	23.10	26.40	29.70	33.00
10 DIRHAMS	1299-1336	24.90	900	22.40	0.72	.72	1.44	2.88	4.32	5.76	7.20	14.40	21.60	28.80	36.00	43.20	50.40	57.60	64.80	72.00
5 FRANCS	1347-1352	5.00	680	3.40	0.11	.11	.22	.44	.66	.88	1.10	2.20	3.30	4.40	5.50	6.60	7.70	8.80	9.90	11.00
10 FRANCS	1347-1352	10.00	680	6.80	0.22	.22	.44	.88	1.32	1.76	2.20	4.40	6.60	8.80	11.00	13.20	15.40	17.60	19.80	22.00
20 FRANCS	1347-1352	20.00	680	13.60	0.44	.44	.88	1.76	2.64	3.52	4.40	8.80	13.20	17.60	22.00	26.40	30.80	35.20	39.60	44.00
100 FRANCS	1372	4.50	720	3.20	0.10	.10	.20	.40	.60	.80	1.00	2.00	3.00	4.00	5.00	6.00	7.00	8.00	9.00	10.00
200 FRANCS	1372	9.00	720	6.50	0.21	.21	.42	.84	1.26	1.68	2.10	4.20	6.30	8.40	10.50	12.60	14.70	16.80	18.90	21.00
500 FRANCS	1376	22.50	900	20.30	0.65	.65	1.30	2.60	3.90	5.20	6.50	13.00	19.50	26.00	32.50	39.00	45.50	52.00	58.50	65.00
1 DIRHAM	1960	6.00	720	4.30	0.14	.14	.28	.56	.84	1.12	1.40	2.80	4.20	5.60	7.00	8.40	9.80	11.20	12.60	14.00
5 DIRHAMS	1965	11.80	720	8.50	0.27	.27	.54	1.08	1.62	2.16	2.70	5.40	8.10	10.80	13.50	16.20	18.90	21.60	24.30	27.00
50 DIRHAMS	1975	35.50	925	32.80	1.05	1.05	2.10	4.20	6.30	8.40	10.50	21.00	31.50	42.00	52.50	63.00	73.50	84.00	94.50	105.00

ALL ABOVE DATES ARE AH DATES.

Coin Denomination	Years of Issue	Coin Wt. Grams	Purity	Silver Wt. Grams	Silver Troy Oz.	Silver Value—U.S. Dollars														
						$1	$2	$4	$6	$8	$10	$20	$30	$40	$50	$60	$70	$80	$90	$100
MOZAMBIQUE																				
2-1/2 ESCUDOS	1935-1951	3.50	650	2.30	0.07	.07	.14	.28	.42	.56	.70	1.40	2.10	2.80	3.50	4.20	4.90	5.60	6.30	7.00
5 ESCUDOS	1935-1949	7.00	650	4.60	0.15	.15	.30	.60	.90	1.20	1.50	3.00	4.50	6.00	7.50	9.00	10.50	12.00	13.50	15.00
5 ESCUDOS	1960	3.50	650	2.30	0.07	.07	.14	.28	.42	.56	.70	1.40	2.10	2.80	3.50	4.20	4.90	5.60	6.30	7.00
10 ESCUDOS	1936-1938	12.50	835	10.40	0.33	.33	.66	1.32	1.98	2.64	3.30	6.60	9.90	13.20	16.50	19.80	23.10	26.40	29.70	33.00
10 ESCUDOS	1952-1960	7.00	720	5.00	0.16	.16	.32	.64	.96	1.28	1.60	3.20	4.80	6.40	8.00	9.60	11.20	12.80	14.40	16.00
10 ESCUDOS	1966	5.00	680	3.40	0.11	.11	.22	.44	.66	.88	1.10	2.20	3.30	4.40	5.50	6.60	7.70	8.80	9.90	11.00
20 ESCUDOS	1952-1960	10.00	720	7.20	0.23	.23	.46	.92	1.38	1.84	2.30	4.60	6.90	9.20	11.50	13.80	16.10	18.40	20.70	23.00
20 ESCUDOS	1966	10.00	680	6.80	0.22	.22	.44	.88	1.32	1.76	2.20	4.40	6.60	8.80	11.00	13.20	15.40	17.60	19.80	22.00
MUSCAT-OMAN																				
1/2 SAIDI-RIYAL	1961-1962	14.00	500	7.00	0.23	.23	.46	.92	1.38	1.84	2.30	4.60	6.90	9.20	11.50	13.80	16.10	18.40	20.70	23.00
1 SAIDI-RIYAL	1959	28.10	833	23.40	0.75	.75	1.50	3.00	4.50	6.00	7.50	15.00	22.50	30.00	37.50	45.00	52.50	60.00	67.50	75.00
1 SAIDI-RIYAL	1959	28.10	500	14.00	0.45	.45	.90	1.80	2.70	3.60	4.50	9.00	13.50	18.00	22.50	27.00	31.50	36.00	40.50	45.00
NEPAL																				
10 RUPEES	1968	15.60	600	9.40	0.30	.30	.60	1.20	1.80	2.40	3.00	6.00	9.00	12.00	15.00	18.00	21.00	24.00	27.00	30.00
10 RUPEES	1974	8.00	250	2.00	0.06	.06	.12	.24	.36	.48	.60	1.20	1.80	2.40	3.00	3.60	4.20	4.80	5.40	6.00
20 RUPEES	1975	16.00	600	9.60	0.31	.31	.62	1.24	1.86	2.48	3.10	6.20	9.30	12.40	15.50	18.60	21.70	24.80	27.90	31.00
25 RUPEES	1974	17.00	600	10.20	0.33	.33	.66	1.32	1.98	2.64	3.30	6.60	9.90	13.20	16.50	19.80	23.10	26.40	29.70	33.00
25 RUPEES	1974	25.30	500	12.70	0.41	.41	.82	1.64	2.46	3.28	4.10	8.20	12.30	16.40	20.50	24.60	28.70	32.80	36.90	41.00
25 RUPEES	1974-1975	28.30	900	25.50	0.82	.82	1.64	3.28	4.92	6.56	8.20	16.40	24.60	32.80	41.00	49.20	57.40	65.60	73.80	82.00
50 RUPEES	1974-1975	31.70	500	15.80	0.51	.51	1.02	2.04	3.06	4.08	5.10	10.20	15.30	20.40	25.50	30.60	35.70	40.80	45.90	51.00
50 RUPEES	1974-1975	35.00	900	31.50	1.01	1.01	2.02	4.04	6.06	8.08	10.10	20.20	30.30	40.40	50.50	60.60	70.70	80.80	90.90	101.00
NETHERLANDS																				
10 CENTS	1848-1945	1.40	640	0.90	0.03	.03	.06	.12	.18	.24	.30	.60	.90	1.20	1.50	1.80	2.10	2.40	2.70	3.00
25 CENTS	1849-1945	3.60	640	2.30	0.07	.07	.14	.28	.42	.56	.70	1.40	2.10	2.80	3.50	4.20	4.90	5.60	6.30	7.00
1/2 GULDEN	1921-1930	3.00	720	2.20	0.07	.07	.14	.28	.42	.56	.70	1.40	2.10	2.80	3.50	4.20	4.90	5.60	6.30	7.00
1 GULDEN	1922-1940	10.00	720	7.20	0.23	.23	.46	.92	1.38	1.84	2.30	4.60	6.90	9.20	11.50	13.80	16.10	18.40	20.70	23.00
1 GULDEN	1954-1967	6.50	720	4.70	0.15	.15	.30	.60	.90	1.20	1.50	3.00	4.50	6.00	7.50	9.00	10.50	12.00	13.50	15.00
2-1/2 GULDEN	1850-1974	25.00	945	23.60	0.76	.76	1.52	3.04	4.56	6.08	7.60	15.20	22.80	30.40	38.00	45.60	53.20	60.80	68.40	76.00
2-1/2 GULDEN	1929-1940	25.00	720	18.00	0.58	.58	1.16	2.32	3.48	4.64	5.80	11.60	17.40	23.20	29.00	34.80	40.60	46.40	52.20	58.00
2-1/2 GULDEN	1959-1966	15.00	720	10.80	0.35	.35	.70	1.40	2.10	2.80	3.50	7.00	10.50	14.00	17.50	21.00	24.50	28.00	31.50	35.00
10 GULDEN	1970-1973	25.00	720	18.00	0.58	.58	1.16	2.32	3.48	4.64	5.80	11.60	17.40	23.20	29.00	34.80	40.60	46.40	52.20	58.00

Coin Denomination	Years of Issue	Coin Wt. Grams	Purity	Silver Wt. Grams	Silver Troy Oz.	Silver Value—U.S. Dollars														
						$1	$2	$4	$6	$8	$10	$20	$30	$40	$50	$60	$70	$80	$90	$100
NETHERLANDS ANTILLES																				
1/10 GULDEN	1941-1970	1.40	640	0.90	0.03	.03	.06	.12	.18	.24	.30	.60	.90	1.20	1.50	1.80	2.10	2.40	2.70	3.00
1/4 GULDEN	1941-1970	3.60	640	2.30	0.07	.07	.14	.28	.42	.56	.70	1.40	2.10	2.80	3.50	4.20	4.90	5.60	6.30	7.00
	1944																			
1 GULDEN	1952-1970	10.00	720	7.20	0.23	.23	.46	.92	1.38	1.84	2.30	4.60	6.90	9.20	11.50	13.80	16.10	18.40	20.70	23.00
2-1/2 GULDEN	1944,1964	25.00	720	18.00	0.58	.58	1.16	2.32	3.48	4.64	5.80	11.60	17.40	23.20	29.00	34.80	40.60	46.40	52.20	58.00
10 GULDEN	1978	25.00	720	18.00	0.58	.58	1.16	2.32	3.48	4.64	5.80	11.60	17.40	23.20	29.00	34.80	40.60	46.40	52.20	58.00
25 GULDEN	1973-1977	42.10	925	39.00	1.25	1.25	2.50	5.00	7.50	10.00	12.50	25.00	37.50	50.00	62.50	75.00	87.50	100.00	112.50	125.00
NETHERLANDS - INDONESIA																				
1/10 GULDEN	1854-1945	1.30	720	0.90	0.03	.03	.06	.12	.18	.24	.30	.60	.90	1.20	1.50	1.80	2.10	2.40	2.70	3.00
1/4 GULDEN	1854-1945	3.20	720	2.30	0.07	.07	.14	.28	.42	.56	.70	1.40	2.10	2.80	3.50	4.20	4.90	5.60	6.30	7.00
1 GULDEN	1943	10.00	720	7.20	0.23	.23	.46	.92	1.38	1.84	2.30	4.60	6.90	9.20	11.50	13.80	16.10	18.40	20.70	23.00
2-1/2 GULDEN	1943	25.00	720	18.00	0.58	.58	1.16	2.32	3.48	4.64	5.80	11.60	17.40	23.20	29.00	34.80	40.60	46.40	52.20	58.00
NEW HEBRIDES																				
100 FRANCS	1966	25.00	835	20.90	0.67	.67	1.34	2.68	4.02	5.36	6.70	13.40	20.10	26.80	33.50	40.20	46.90	53.60	60.30	67.00
NEW ZEALAND																				
3 PENCE	1933-1965	1.40	500	0.70	0.02	.02	.04	.08	.12	.16	.20	.40	.60	.80	1.00	1.20	1.40	1.60	1.80	2.00
6 PENCE	1933-1965	2.80	500	1.40	0.05	.05	.10	.20	.30	.40	.50	1.00	1.50	2.00	2.50	3.00	3.50	4.00	4.50	5.00
1 SHILLING	1933-1965	5.60	500	2.80	0.09	.09	.18	.36	.54	.72	.90	1.80	2.70	3.60	4.50	5.40	6.30	7.20	8.10	9.00
1 FLORIN	1933-1965	11.30	500	5.70	0.18	.18	.36	.72	1.08	1.44	1.80	3.60	5.40	7.20	9.00	10.80	12.60	14.40	16.20	18.00
1/2 CROWN	1933-1965	14.10	500	7.10	0.23	.23	.46	.92	1.38	1.84	2.30	4.60	6.90	9.20	11.50	13.80	16.10	18.40	20.70	23.00
1 CROWN	1949	28.30	500	14.10	0.45	.45	.90	1.80	2.70	3.60	4.50	9.00	13.50	18.00	22.50	27.00	31.50	36.00	40.50	45.00
1 DOLLAR	1974-1978	28.30	925	26.20	0.84	.84	1.68	3.36	5.04	6.72	8.40	16.80	25.20	33.60	42.00	50.40	58.80	67.20	75.60	84.00
NICARAGUA																				
10 CENTAVOS	1912-1936	2.50	800	2.00	0.06	.06	.12	.24	.36	.48	.60	1.20	1.80	2.40	3.00	3.60	4.20	4.80	5.40	6.00
25 CENTAVOS	1912-1936	6.30	800	5.00	0.16	.16	.32	.64	.96	1.28	1.60	3.20	4.80	6.40	8.00	9.60	11.20	12.80	14.40	16.00
50 CENTAVOS	1912,1929	12.50	800	10.00	0.32	.32	.64	1.28	1.92	2.56	3.20	6.40	9.60	12.80	16.00	19.20	22.40	25.60	28.80	32.00
20 CORDOBAS	1975	5.00	925	4.70	0.15	.15	.30	.60	.90	1.20	1.50	3.00	4.50	6.00	7.50	9.00	10.50	12.00	13.50	15.00
50 CORDOBAS	1975	12.60	925	11.60	0.37	.37	.74	1.48	2.22	2.96	3.70	7.40	11.10	14.80	18.50	22.20	25.90	29.60	33.30	37.00
100 CORDOBAS	1975	23.30	925	21.50	0.69	.69	1.38	2.76	4.14	5.52	6.90	13.80	20.70	27.60	34.50	41.40	48.30	55.20	62.10	69.00

Coin Denomination	Years of Issue	Coin Wt. Grams	Purity	Silver Wt. Grams	Silver Troy Oz.	Silver Value—U.S. Dollars														
						$1	$2	$4	$6	$8	$10	$20	$30	$40	$50	$60	$70	$80	$90	$100
NIGER																				
500 FRANCS	1960	10.00	900	9.00	0.29	.29	.58	1.16	1.74	2.32	2.90	5.80	8.70	11.60	14.50	17.40	18.90	23.20	26.10	29.00
1000 FRANCS	1960	20.00	900	18.00	0.58	.58	1.16	2.32	3.48	4.64	5.80	11.60	17.40	23.20	29.00	34.80	40.60	46.40	52.20	58.00
NIGERIA - BIAFRA																				
1 POUND	1969	28.30	925	26.20	0.84	.84	1.68	3.36	5.04	6.72	8.40	16.80	25.20	33.60	42.00	50.40	58.80	67.20	75.60	84.00
NORWAY																				
10 ORE	1874-1919	1.50	400	0.60	0.02	.02	.04	.08	.12	.16	.20	.40	.60	.80	1.00	1.20	1.40	1.60	1.80	2.00
25 ORE	1876-1919	2.40	600	1.50	0.05	.05	.10	.20	.30	.40	.50	1.00	1.50	2.00	2.50	3.00	3.50	4.00	4.50	5.00
50 ORE	1874-1919	5.00	600	3.00	0.10	.10	.20	.40	.60	.80	1.00	2.00	3.00	4.00	5.00	6.00	7.00	8.00	9.00	10.00
1 KRONE	1875-1917	7.50	800	6.00	0.19	.19	.38	.76	1.14	1.52	1.90	3.80	5.70	7.60	9.50	11.40	13.30	15.20	17.10	19.00
2 KRONER	1964	21.00	900	18.90	0.61	.61	1.22	2.44	3.66	4.88	6.10	12.20	18.30	24.40	30.50	36.60	42.70	48.00	54.90	61.00
25 KRONER	1970	29.00	900	26.10	0.84	.84	1.68	3.36	5.04	6.72	8.40	16.80	25.20	33.60	42.00	50.40	58.80	67.20	75.60	84.00
50 KRONER	1978	27.00	925	25.00	0.80	.80	1.60	3.20	4.80	6.40	8.00	16.00	24.00	32.00	40.00	48.00	56.00	64.00	72.00	80.00
OMAN																				
1 OMANI-RIAL	1978	15.00	500	7.50	0.24	.24	.48	.96	1.44	1.92	2.40	4.80	7.20	9.60	12.00	14.40	16.80	19.20	21.60	24.00
2-1/2 " RIAL	1977	28.30	925	26.20	0.84	.84	1.68	3.36	5.04	6.72	8.40	16.80	25.20	33.60	42.00	50.40	58.80	67.20	75.60	84.00
5 OMANI-RIAL	1977	35.00	925	32.40	1.04	1.04	2.08	4.16	6.24	8.32	10.40	20.80	31.20	41.60	52.00	62.40	72.80	83.20	93.60	104.00
PAKISTAN																				
100 RUPEES	1976-1977	28.30	925	26.20	0.84	.84	1.68	3.36	5.04	6.72	8.40	16.80	25.20	33.60	42.00	50.40	58.80	67.20	75.60	84.00
150 RUPEES	1976	35.00	925	32.40	1.04	1.04	2.08	4.16	6.24	8.32	10.40	20.80	31.20	41.60	52.00	62.40	72.80	83.20	93.60	104.00
PANAMA																				
2-1/2 CENTESIMOS	1904	1.30	900	1.20	0.04	.04	.08	.16	.24	.32	.40	.80	1.20	1.60	2.00	2.40	2.80	3.20	3.60	4.00
5 CENTESIMOS	1904	2.50	900	2.30	0.07	.07	.14	.28	.42	.56	.70	1.40	2.10	2.80	3.50	4.20	4.90	5.60	6.30	7.00
10 CENTESIMOS	1904	5.00	900	4.50	0.14	.14	.28	.56	.84	1.12	1.40	2.80	4.20	5.60	7.00	8.40	9.80	11.20	12.60	14.00

Coin Denomination	Years of Issue	Coin Wt. Grams	Purity	Silver Wt. Grams	Silver Troy Oz.	Silver Value—U.S. Dollars														
						$1	$2	$4	$6	$8	$10	$20	$30	$40	$50	$60	$70	$80	$90	$100
PANAMA - CONT'D.																				
25 CENTESIMOS	1904	12.50	900	11.30	0.36	.36	.72	1.44	2.16	2.88	3.60	7.20	10.80	14.40	18.00	21.60	25.20	28.80	32.40	36.00
50 CENTESIMOS	1904	25.00	900	22.50	0.72	.72	1.44	2.88	4.32	5.76	7.20	14.40	21.60	28.80	37.00	43.20	50.40	57.60	64.80	72.00
1/10 BALBOA	1930-1962	2.50	900	2.30	0.07	.07	.14	.28	.42	.56	.70	1.40	2.10	2.80	3.50	4.20	4.90	5.60	6.30	7.00
1/4 BALBOA	1930-1962	6.30	900	5.60	0.18	.18	.36	.72	1.08	1.44	1.80	3.60	5.40	7.20	9.00	10.80	12.60	14.40	16.20	18.00
1/2 BALBOA	1931-1962	12.50	900	11.30	0.36	.36	.72	1.44	2.16	2.88	3.60	7.20	10.80	14.40	18.00	21.60	25.20	28.80	32.40	36.00
1 BALBOA	1931-1974	26.80	900	24.10	0.77	.77	1.54	2.88	4.62	6.16	7.70	15.40	23.10	28.80	38.50	46.20	53.90	61.60	69.30	77.00
1 BALBOA	1975-1979	26.80	925	24.80	0.80	.80	1.60	3.20	4.80	6.40	8.00	16.00	24.00	32.00	40.00	48.00	56.00	64.00	72.00	80.00
5 BALBOA	1970-1979	35.10	925	32.50	1.04	1.04	2.08	4.16	6.24	8.32	10.40	20.80	31.20	41.60	52.00	62.40	72.80	83.20	93.60	104.00
10 BALBOA	1978-1979	42.50	925	39.30	1.26	1.26	2.52	5.04	7.56	10.08	12.60	25.20	37.80	50.40	63.00	75.60	88.20	100.80	113.40	126.00
20 BALBOA	1971-1978	129.60	925	119.90	3.86	3.86	7.72	15.44	23.16	30.88	38.60	77.20	115.80	154.40	193.00	231.60	270.20	308.80	347.40	386.00
PAPUA - NEW GUINEA																				
1 SHILLING	1935-1945	5.60	925	5.20	0.17	.17	.34	.68	1.02	1.36	1.70	3.40	5.10	6.80	8.50	10.20	11.90	13.60	15.30	17.00
5 KINA	1975-1977	26.80	500	13.40	0.43	.43	.86	1.72	2.58	3.44	4.30	8.60	12.90	17.20	21.50	25.80	30.10	34.40	38.70	43.00
10 KINA	1975-1978	41.30	925	38.20	1.23	1.23	2.46	4.92	7.38	9.84	12.30	24.60	36.90	49.20	61.50	73.80	86.10	98.40	110.70	246.00
PARAGUAY																				
150 GUARANIES	1972-1975	25.00	1000	25.00	0.80	.80	1.60	3.20	4.80	6.40	8.00	16.00	24.00	32.00	40.00	48.00	56.00	64.00	72.00	80.00
300 GUARANIES	1968	26.80	900	24.10	0.77	.77	1.54	3.08	4.62	6.16	7.70	15.40	23.10	30.80	38.50	46.20	53.90	61.60	69.30	77.00
PERU																				
1/2 DINERO	1863-1917	1.30	900	1.10	0.04	.04	.08	.16	.24	.32	.40	.80	1.20	1.60	2.00	2.40	2.80	3.20	3.60	4.00
1 DINERO	1863-1919	2.50	900	2.30	0.07	.07	.14	.28	.42	.56	.70	1.40	2.10	2.80	3.50	4.20	4.90	5.60	6.30	7.00
1/5 SOL	1863-1917	5.00	900	4.50	0.14	.14	.28	.56	.84	1.12	1.40	2.80	4.20	5.60	7.00	8.40	9.80	11.20	12.60	14.00
1/2 SOL	1863-1917	12.50	900	11.30	0.36	.36	.72	1.44	2.16	2.88	3.60	7.20	10.80	14.40	18.00	21.60	25.20	28.80	32.40	36.00
1/2 SOL	1922-1935	12.50	500	6.30	0.20	.20	.40	.80	1.20	1.60	2.00	4.00	6.00	8.00	10.00	12.00	14.00	16.00	18.00	20.00
1 SOL	1863-1916	25.00	900	22.30	0.72	.72	1.44	2.88	4.32	5.76	7.20	14.40	21.60	28.80	36.00	43.20	50.40	57.60	64.80	72.00
1 SOL	1923-1935	25.00	500	12.50	0.40	.40	.80	1.60	2.40	3.20	4.00	8.00	12.00	16.00	20.00	24.00	28.00	32.00	36.00	40.00
5 PESETAS	1880-1882	25.00	900	22.50	0.72	.72	1.44	2.88	4.32	5.76	7.20	14.40	21.60	28.80	36.00	43.20	50.40	57.60	64.80	72.00
20 SOLES	1965-1966	8.00	900	7.20	0.23	.23	.46	.92	1.38	1.84	2.30	4.60	6.90	9.20	11.50	13.80	16.10	18.40	20.70	23.00
50 SOLES	1971	22.00	800	17.60	0.57	.57	1.14	2.28	3.42	4.56	5.70	11.40	17.10	22.80	28.50	34.20	39.90	45.60	51.30	57.00
100 SOLES	1973	21.50	800	17.20	0.55	.55	1.10	2.20	3.30	4.40	5.50	11.00	16.50	22.00	27.50	33.00	38.50	44.00	49.50	55.00
200 SOLES	1974-1977	22.00	800	17.60	0.57	.57	1.14	2.28	3.42	4.56	5.70	11.40	17.10	22.80	28.50	34.20	39.90	45.60	51.30	57.00
400 SOLES	1976	27.90	900	25.10	0.81	.81	1.62	3.24	4.86	6.48	8.10	16.20	24.30	32.40	40.50	48.60	56.70	64.80	72.90	81.00
1000 SOLES	1979	15.60	500	7.80	0.25	.25	.50	1.00	1.50	2.00	2.50	5.00	7.50	10.00	12.50	15.00	17.50	20.00	22.50	25.00
5000 SOLES	1979	33.50	925	30.90	0.99	.99	1.98	3.96	5.94	7.92	9.90	19.80	29.70	39.60	49.50	59.40	69.30	79.20	89.10	99.00

Coin Denomination	Years of Issue	Coin Wt. Grams	Purity	Silver Wt. Grams	Silver Troy Oz.	Silver Value—U.S. Dollars														
						$1	$2	$4	$6	$8	$10	$20	$30	$40	$50	$60	$70	$80	$90	$100
PHILIPPINES																				
10 CENTAVOS	1903-1904	2.70	900	2.40	0.08	.08	.16	.32	.48	.64	.80	1.60	2.40	3.20	4.00	4.80	5.60	6.40	7.20	8.00
10 CENTAVOS	1907-1945	2.00	750	1.50	0.05	.05	.10	.20	.30	.40	.50	1.00	1.50	2.00	2.50	3.00	3.50	4.00	4.50	5.00
20 CENTAVOS	1903-1905	5.40	900	4.80	0.15	.15	.30	.60	.90	1.20	1.50	3.00	4.50	6.00	7.50	9.00	10.50	12.00	13.50	15.00
20 CENTAVOS	1907-1945	4.00	750	3.00	0.10	.10	.20	.40	.60	.80	1.00	2.00	3.00	4.00	5.00	6.00	7.00	8.00	9.00	10.00
50 CENTAVOS	1903-1905	13.50	900	12.10	0.39	.39	.78	1.56	2.34	3.12	3.90	7.80	11.70	15.60	19.50	23.40	27.30	31.20	35.10	39.00
50 CENTAVOS	1907-1945	10.00	750	7.50	0.24	.24	.48	.96	1.44	1.92	2.40	4.80	7.20	9.60	12.00	14.40	16.80	19.20	21.60	24.00
50 CENTAVOS	1947	10.00	800	8.00	0.26	.26	.52	1.04	1.56	2.08	2.60	5.20	7.80	10.40	13.00	15.60	18.20	20.80	23.40	26.00
1/2 PESO	1961	10.00	900	9.00	0.29	.29	.58	1.16	1.74	2.32	2.90	5.80	8.70	11.60	14.50	17.40	18.90	23.20	26.10	29.00
1 PESO	1903-1905	27.00	900	24.30	0.78	.78	1.56	3.12	4.68	6.24	7.80	15.60	23.40	31.20	39.00	46.80	54.60	62.40	70.20	78.00
1 PESO	1907-1947	20.00	800	16.00	0.51	.51	1.02	2.04	3.06	4.08	5.10	10.20	15.30	20.40	25.50	30.60	35.70	40.80	45.90	51.00
1 PESO	1961-1967	26.70	900	24.10	0.77	.77	1.54	3.08	4.62	6.16	7.70	15.40	23.10	30.80	38.50	46.20	53.90	61.60	69.30	77.00
1 PISO	1969-1970	26.70	900	24.10	0.77	.77	1.54	3.08	4.62	6.16	7.70	15.40	23.10	30.80	38.50	46.20	53.90	61.60	69.30	77.00
25 PISO	1974-1978	27.00	500	13.50	0.43	.43	.86	1.72	2.58	3.44	4.30	8.60	12.90	17.20	21.50	25.80	30.10	34.40	38.70	43.00
50 PISO	1975-1978	28.00	925	25.90	0.83	.83	1.66	3.32	4.98	6.64	8.30	16.60	24.90	33.20	41.50	49.80	58.10	66.40	74.70	83.00
POLAND																				
1 ZLOTY	1924-1925	5.00	750	3.80	0.12	.12	.24	.48	.72	.96	1.20	2.40	3.60	4.80	6.00	7.20	8.40	9.60	10.80	11.20
2 ZLOTY	1924-1936	10.00	750	7.50	0.24	.24	.48	.96	1.44	1.92	2.40	4.80	7.20	9.60	12.00	14.40	16.80	19.20	21.60	24.00
2 ZLOTY	1932-1934	4.40	750	3.30	0.11	.11	.22	.44	.66	.88	1.10	2.20	3.30	4.40	5.50	6.60	7.70	8.80	9.90	11.00
5 ZLOTYCH	1928-1932	18.00	750	13.50	0.43	.43	.86	1.72	2.58	3.44	4.30	8.60	12.90	17.20	21.50	25.80	30.10	34.40	38.70	43.00
5 ZLOTY	1932-1938	11.00	750	8.30	0.27	.27	.54	1.08	1.62	2.16	2.70	5.40	8.10	10.80	13.50	16.20	18.90	21.60	24.30	27.00
10 ZLOTYCH	1932-1939	22.00	750	16.50	0.53	.53	1.06	2.12	3.18	4.24	5.30	10.60	15.90	21.20	26.50	31.80	37.10	42.40	47.70	53.00
50 ZLOTYCH	1972	12.60	750	9.50	0.31	.31	.62	1.24	1.86	2.48	3.10	6.20	9.30	12.40	15.50	18.60	21.70	24.80	27.90	31.00
100 ZLOTYCH	1966	20.10	900	18.10	0.58	.58	1.16	2.32	3.48	4.64	5.80	11.60	17.40	23.20	29.00	34.80	40.60	46.40	52.20	58.00
100 ZLOTYCH	1973-1979	13.60	625	8.50	0.27	.27	.54	1.08	1.62	2.16	2.70	5.40	8.10	10.80	13.50	16.20	18.90	21.60	24.30	27.00
200 ZLOTYCH	1974-1979	14.50	625	9.10	0.29	.29	.58	1.16	1.74	2.32	2.90	5.80	8.70	11.60	14.50	17.40	18.90	23.20	26.10	29.00
PORTUGAL																				
100 REIS	1838-1898	2.50	917	2.30	0.07	.07	.14	.28	.42	.56	.70	1.40	2.10	2.80	3.50	4.20	4.90	5.60	6.30	7.00
200 REIS	1838-1898	5.00	917	4.60	0.15	.15	.30	.60	.90	1.20	1.50	3.00	4.50	6.00	7.50	9.00	10.50	12.00	13.50	15.00
200 REIS	1909	5.00	835	4.20	0.14	.14	.28	.56	.84	1.12	1.40	2.80	4.20	5.60	7.00	8.40	9.80	11.20	12.60	14.00
500 REIS	1837-1910	12.50	917	11.50	0.37	.37	.74	1.48	2.22	2.96	3.70	7.40	11.10	14.80	18.50	22.20	25.90	29.60	33.30	37.00
1000 REIS	1898-1910	25.00	917	22.30	0.72	.72	1.44	2.88	4.32	5.76	7.20	14.40	21.60	28.80	36.00	43.20	50.40	57.60	64.80	72.00
10 CENTAVOS	1915	2.50	835	2.10	0.07	.07	.14	.28	.42	.56	.70	1.40	2.10	2.80	3.50	4.20	4.90	5.60	6.30	7.00
20 CENTAVOS	1913,1916	5.00	835	4.20	0.14	.14	.28	.56	.84	1.12	1.40	2.80	4.20	5.60	7.00	8.40	9.80	11.20	12.60	14.00
50 CENTAVOS	1912-1916	12.50	835	10.40	0.33	.33	.66	1.32	1.98	2.64	3.30	6.60	9.90	13.20	16.50	19.80	23.10	26.40	29.70	33.00
1 ESCUDO	1910-1916	25.00	835	28.90	0.93	.93	1.86	3.72	5.58	7.44	9.30	18.60	27.90	37.20	46.50	55.80	65.10	74.40	83.70	93.00
2-1/2 ESCUDO	1932-1951	3.50	650	2.30	0.07	.07	.14	.28	.42	.56	.70	1.40	2.10	2.80	3.50	4.20	4.90	5.60	6.30	7.00

Coin Denomination	Years of Issue	Coin Wt. Grams	Purity	Silver Wt. Grams	Silver Troy Oz.	Silver Value—U.S. Dollars														
						$1	$2	$4	$6	$8	$10	$20	$30	$40	$50	$60	$70	$80	$90	$100
PORTUGAL - CONT'D.																				
5 ESCUDOS	1932-1960	7.00	650	4.60	0.15	.15	.30	.60	.90	1.20	1.50	3.00	4.50	6.00	7.50	9.00	10.50	12.00	13.50	15.00
10 ESCUDOS	1928-1955	12.50	835	10.40	0.33	.33	.66	1.32	1.98	2.64	3.30	6.60	9.90	13.20	16.50	19.80	23.10	26.40	29.70	33.00
10 ESCUDOS	1960	12.50	680	8.50	0.27	.27	.54	1.08	1.62	2.16	2.70	5.40	8.10	10.80	13.50	16.20	18.90	21.60	24.30	27.00
20 ESCUDOS	1953,1960	21.00	800	16.80	0.54	.54	1.08	2.16	3.24	4.32	5.40	10.80	16.20	21.60	27.00	32.40	37.80	43.20	48.60	54.00
20 ESCUDOS	1966	10.00	900	9.00	0.29	.29	.58	1.16	1.74	2.32	2.90	5.80	8.70	11.60	14.50	17.40	18.90	23.20	26.10	29.00
50 ESCUDOS	1968-1972	18.00	650	11.70	0.38	.38	.76	1.52	2.28	3.04	3.80	7.60	11.40	15.20	19.00	22.80	26.60	30.40	34.20	38.00
100 ESCUDOS	1974	18.00	650	11.70	0.38	.38	.76	1.52	2.28	3.04	3.80	7.60	11.40	15.20	19.00	22.80	26.60	30.40	34.20	38.00
250 ESCUDOS	1974	24.00	900	21.60	0.69	.69	1.38	2.76	4.14	5.52	6.90	13.80	20.70	27.60	34.50	41.40	48.30	55.20	62.10	69.00
PORTUGESE INDIA																				
1/4 RUPIA	1881	1.50	916	1.30	0.04	.04	.08	.16	.24	.32	.40	.80	1.20	1.60	2.00	2.40	2.80	3.20	3.60	4.00
1/2 RUPIA	1881-1886	5.80	916	5.30	0.17	.17	.34	.68	1.02	1.36	1.70	3.40	5.10	6.80	8.50	10.20	11.90	13.60	15.30	17.00
1 RUPIA	1881-1935	11.70	916	10.70	0.34	.34	.68	1.36	2.04	2.72	3.40	6.80	10.20	13.60	17.00	20.40	23.80	27.20	30.60	34.00
RAS AL KHAIMA																				
1 RIYAL	1969	3.90	640	2.50	0.08	.08	.16	.32	.48	.64	.80	1.60	2.40	3.20	4.00	4.80	5.60	6.40	7.20	8.00
2 RIYALS	1969	6.50	835	5.40	0.17	.17	.34	.68	1.02	1.36	1.70	3.40	5.10	6.80	8.50	10.20	11.90	13.60	15.30	17.00
2-1/2 RIYALS	1970	7.00	925	6.50	0.21	.21	.42	.84	1.26	1.68	2.10	4.20	6.30	8.40	10.50	12.60	14.70	16.80	18.90	21.00
5 RIYALS	1970	15.00	835	12.50	0.40	.40	.80	1.60	2.40	3.20	4.00	8.00	12.00	16.00	20.00	24.00	28.00	32.00	36.00	40.00
7-1/2 RIYALS	1970	22.30	925	20.60	0.66	.66	1.32	2.64	3.96	5.28	6.60	13.20	19.80	26.40	33.00	39.60	46.20	52.80	59.40	66.00
10 RIYALS	1970	30.00	925	27.70	0.89	.89	1.78	3.56	5.34	7.12	8.90	17.80	26.70	35.60	44.50	53.40	62.30	71.20	70.10	89.00
15 RIYALS	1970	44.90	925	41.50	1.33	1.33	2.66	5.32	7.98	10.64	13.30	26.60	39.90	53.20	66.50	79.80	93.10	106.40	119.70	133.00
RHODESIA																				
3 PENCE	1932-1942	1.40	925	1.30	0.04	.04	.08	.16	.24	.32	.40	.80	1.20	1.60	2.00	2.40	2.80	3.20	3.60	4.00
3 P3NCE	1944-1946, 1955	1.40	500	0.70	0.02	.02	.04	.08	.12	.16	.20	.40	.60	.80	1.00	1.20	1.40	1.60	1.80	2.00
6 PENCE	1932-1942	2.80	925	2.60	0.08	.08	.16	.32	.48	.64	.80	1.60	2.40	3.20	4.00	4.80	5.60	6.40	7.20	8.00
6 PENCE	1944-1946, 1955	2.80	500	1.40	0.05	.05	.10	.20	.30	.40	.50	1.00	1.50	2.00	2.50	3.00	3.50	4.00	4.50	5.00
1 SHILLING	1932-1942	5.70	925	5.20	0.17	.17	.34	.68	1.02	1.36	1.70	3.40	5.10	6.80	8.50	10.20	11.90	13.60	15.30	17.00
1 SHILLING	1944-1946, 1955	5.70	500	2.80	0.09	.09	.18	.36	.54	.72	.90	1.80	2.70	3.60	4.50	5.40	6.30	7.20	8.10	9.00
2 SHILLINGS	1932-1942	11.30	925	10.50	0.34	.34	.68	1.36	2.04	2.72	3.40	6.80	10.20	13.60	17.00	20.40	23.80	27.20	30.60	34.00
2 SHILLINGS	1944-1946, 1955	11.30	500	5.70	0.18	.18	.36	.72	1.08	1.44	1.80	3.60	5.40	7.20	9.00	10.80	12.60	14.40	16.20	18.00

Coin Denomination	Years of Issue	Coin Wt. Grams	Purity	Silver Wt. Grams	Silver Troy Oz.	Silver Value—U.S. Dollars $1	$2	$4	$6	$8	$10	$20	$30	$40	$50	$60	$70	$80	$90	$100
RHODESIA - CONT'D.																				
1/2 CROWN	1932-1942 1944-1946	14.10	925	13.10	0.42	.42	.84	1.68	2.52	3.36	4.20	8.40	12.60	16.80	21.00	25.20	29.40	33.60	37.80	42.00
1/2 CROWN	1955	14.10	500	7.10	0.23	.23	.46	.92	1.38	1.84	2.30	4.60	6.90	9.20	11.50	13.80	16.10	18.40	20.70	23.00
1 CROWN	1953	28.30	500	14.10	0.45	.45	.90	1.80	2.70	3.60	4.50	9.00	13.50	18.00	22.50	27.00	31.50	36.00	40.50	45.00
ROUMANIA																				
50 BANI	1873-1914	2.50	835	2.10	0.07	.07	.14	.28	.42	.56	.70	1.40	2.10	2.80	3.50	4.20	4.90	5.60	6.30	7.00
1 LEU	1870-1914	5.00	835	4.20	0.14	.14	.28	.56	.84	1.12	1.40	2.80	4.20	5.60	7.00	8.40	9.80	11.20	12.60	14.00
2 LEI	1872-1914	10.00	835	8.40	0.27	.27	.54	1.08	1.62	2.16	2.70	5.40	8.10	10.80	13.50	16.20	18.90	21.60	24.30	27.00
5 LEI	1880-1906	25.00	900	22.50	0.72	.72	1.44	2.88	4.32	5.76	7.20	14.40	21.60	28.80	36.00	43.20	50.40	57.60	64.80	72.00
100 LEI	1932	12.00	500	6.00	0.19	.19	.38	.76	1.14	1.52	1.90	3.80	5.70	7.60	9.50	11.40	13.30	15.20	17.10	19.00
200 LEI	1942	6.00	500	3.00	0.10	.10	.20	.40	.60	.80	1.00	2.00	3.00	4.00	5.00	6.00	7.00	8.00	9.00	10.00
250 LEI	1935	13.50	750	10.10	0.32	.32	.64	1.28	1.92	2.56	3.20	6.40	9.60	12.80	16.00	19.20	22.40	25.60	28.80	32.00
250 LEI	1939-1940	12.00	750	9.00	0.29	.29	.58	1.16	1.74	2.32	2.90	5.80	8.70	11.60	14.50	17.40	18.90	23.20	26.10	29.00
500 LEI	1941	24.90	835	20.80	0.67	.67	1.34	2.68	4.02	5.36	6.70	13.40	20.10	26.80	33.50	40.20	46.90	53.60	60.30	67.00
500 LEI	1944	11.90	835	9.90	0.32	.32	.64	1.28	1.92	2.56	3.20	6.40	9.60	12.80	16.00	19.20	22.40	25.60	28.80	32.00
25,000 LEI	1946	12.30	500	6.20	0.20	.20	.40	.80	1.20	1.60	2.00	4.00	6.00	8.00	10.00	12.00	14.00	16.00	18.00	20.00
100,000 LEI	1946	25.00	500	12.50	0.40	.40	.80	1.60	2.40	3.20	4.00	8.00	12.00	16.00	20.00	24.00	28.00	32.00	36.00	40.00
RUSSIA																				
5 KOPEKS	1813-1860	0.90	868	0.80	0.03	.03	.06	.12	.18	.24	.30	.60	.90	1.20	1.50	1.80	2.10	2.40	2.70	3.00
5 KOPEKS	1860-1915	0.90	750	0.70	0.02	.02	.04	.08	.12	.16	.20	.40	.60	.80	1.00	1.20	1.40	1.60	1.80	2.00
10 KOPEKS	1859-1866	1.80	750	1.40	0.05	.05	.10	.20	.30	.40	.50	1.00	1.50	2.00	2.50	3.00	3.50	4.00	4.50	5.00
10 KOPEKS	1867-1931	1.80	500	0.90	0.03	.03	.06	.12	.18	.24	.30	.60	.90	1.20	1.50	1.80	2.10	2.40	2.70	3.00
15 KOPEKS	1860-1866	2.70	750	2.00	0.06	.06	.12	.24	.36	.48	.60	1.20	1.80	2.40	3.00	3.60	4.20	4.80	5.40	6.00
15 KOPEKS	1867-1931	2.70	500	1.40	0.05	.05	.10	.20	.30	.40	.50	1.00	1.50	2.00	2.50	3.00	3.50	4.00	4.50	5.00
20 KOPEKS	1859-1866	3.60	750	2.70	0.09	.09	.18	.36	.54	.72	.90	1.80	2.70	3.60	4.50	5.40	6.30	7.20	8.10	9.00
20 KOPEKS	1867-1931	3.60	500	1.80	0.06	.06	.12	.24	.36	.48	.60	1.20	1.80	2.40	3.00	3.60	4.20	4.80	5.40	6.00
25 KOPEKS	1855-1885	5.00	868	4.30	0.14	.14	.28	.56	.84	1.12	1.40	2.80	4.20	5.60	7.00	8.40	9.80	11.20	12.60	14.00
25 KOPEKS	1886-1901	5.00	900	4.50	0.14	.14	.28	.56	.84	1.12	1.40	2.80	4.20	5.60	7.00	8.40	9.80	11.20	12.60	14.00
50 KOPEKS	1886-1927	10.00	900	9.00	0.29	.29	.58	1.16	1.74	2.32	2.90	5.80	8.70	11.60	14.50	17.40	18.90	23.20	26.10	29.00
1 ROUBLE	1886-1924	20.00	900	18.00	0.58	.58	1.16	2.32	3.48	4.64	5.80	11.60	17.40	23.20	29.00	34.80	40.60	46.40	52.20	58.00
5 ROUBLES	1977-1980	16.70	900	15.00	0.48	.48	.96	1.92	2.88	3.84	4.80	9.60	14.40	19.20	24.00	28.80	33.60	38.40	43.20	48.00
10 ROUBLES	1977-1980	33.30	900	30.00	0.96	.96	1.92	3.84	5.76	7.68	9.60	19.20	28.80	38.40	48.00	57.60	67.20	76.80	86.40	96.00
RWANDA																				
200 FRANCS	1972	18.60	800	14.90	0.48	.48	.96	1.92	2.88	3.84	4.80	9.60	14.40	19.20	24.00	28.80	33.60	38.40	43.20	48.00

Coin Denomination	Years of Issue	Coin Wt. Grams	Purity	Silver Wt. Grams	Silver Troy Oz.	Silver Value—U.S. Dollars														
						$1	$2	$4	$6	$8	$10	$20	$30	$40	$50	$60	$70	$80	$90	$100
ST. HELENA																				
25 PENCE	1973-1977	28.30	925	26.20	0.84	.84	1.68	3.36	5.04	6.72	8.40	16.80	25.20	33.60	42.00	50.40	58.80	67.20	75.60	84.00
1 CROWN	1978	28.30	925	26.20	0.84	.84	1.68	3.36	5.04	6.72	8.40	16.80	25.20	33.60	42.00	50.40	58.80	67.20	75.60	84.00
ST. THOMAS AND PRINCE ISLANDS																				
2-1/2 ESCUDOS	1939-1951	3.50	650	2.30	0.07	.07	.14	.28	.42	.56	.70	1.40	2.10	2.80	3.50	4.20	4.90	5.60	6.30	7.00
5 ESCUDOS	1939-1962	7.00	650	4.60	0.15	.15	.30	.60	.90	1.20	1.50	3.00	4.50	6.00	7.50	9.00	10.50	12.00	13.50	15.00
10 ESCUDOS	1939	12.50	835	10.40	0.33	.33	.66	1.32	1.98	2.64	3.30	6.60	9.90	13.20	16.50	19.80	23.10	26.40	29.70	33.00
10 ESCUDOS	1951	12.50	720	9.00	0.29	.29	.58	1.16	1.74	2.32	2.90	5.80	8.70	11.60	14.50	17.40	18.90	23.20	26.10	29.00
50 ESCUDOS	1970	18.00	650	11.70	0.38	.38	.76	1.52	2.28	3.04	3.80	7.60	11.40	15.20	19.00	22.80	26.60	30.40	34.20	38.00
SAN MARINO																				
50 CENTESIMI	1898	2.50	835	2.10	0.07	.07	.14	.28	.42	.56	.70	1.40	2.10	2.80	3.50	4.20	4.90	5.40	6.30	7.00
1 LIRA	1898,1906	5.00	835	4.20	0.14	.14	.28	.56	.84	1.12	1.40	2.80	4.20	5.60	7.00	8.40	9.80	11.20	12.60	14.00
1 LIRE	1898,1906	10.00	835	8.40	0.27	.27	.54	1.08	1.62	2.16	2.70	5.40	8.10	10.80	13.50	16.20	18.90	21.60	24.30	27.00
5 LIRE	1931-1938	5.00	835	4.20	0.14	.14	.28	.56	.84	1.12	1.40	2.80	4.20	5.60	7.00	8.40	9.80	11.20	12.60	14.00
10 LIRE	1931-1938	10.00	835	8.40	0.27	.27	.54	1.08	1.62	2.16	2.70	5.40	8.10	10.80	13.50	16.20	18.90	21.60	24.30	27.00
500 LIRE	1972-1978	11.00	835	9.20	0.30	.30	.60	1.20	1.80	2.40	3.00	6.00	9.00	12.00	15.00	18.00	21.00	24.00	27.00	30.00
1000 LIRE	1977-1978	14.60	835	12.20	0.39	.39	.78	1.56	2.34	3.12	3.90	7.80	11.70	15.60	19.50	23.40	27.30	31.20	35.10	39.00
SAUDI ARABIA																				
1/4 RIYAL	1354-1374	2.90	917	2.70	0.09	.09	.18	.36	.54	.72	.90	1.80	2.70	3.60	4.50	5.40	6.30	7.20	8.10	9.00
1/2 RIYAL	1354-1374	5.80	917	5.30	0.17	.17	.34	.68	1.02	1.36	1.70	3.40	5.10	6.80	8.50	10.20	11.90	13.60	15.30	17.00
1 RIYAL	1846-1848	11.70	917	10.70	0.34	.34	.68	1.36	2.04	2.72	3.40	6.80	10.20	13.60	17.00	20.40	23.80	27.20	30.60	34.00
DATES ABOVE INCLUDE AH DATES.																				
SEYCHELLES																				
25 CENTS	1939-1944	2.90	917	2.70	0.09	.09	.18	.36	.54	.72	.90	1.80	2.70	3.60	4.50	5.40	6.30	7.20	8.10	9.00
1/2 RUPEE	1939	5.80	500	2.90	0.09	.09	.18	.36	.54	.72	.90	1.80	2.70	3.60	4.50	5.40	6.30	7.20	8.10	9.00
1 RUPEE	1939	11.70	500	5.80	0.19	.19	.38	.76	1.14	1.52	1.90	3.80	5.70	7.60	9.50	11.40	13.30	15.20	17.10	19.00
5 RUPEES	1972-1976	13.50	925	12.50	0.40	.40	.80	1.60	2.40	3.20	4.00	8.00	12.00	16.00	20.00	24.00	28.00	32.00	36.00	40.00
10 RUPEES	1974-1976	28.30	925	26.20	0.84	.84	1.68	3.36	5.04	6.72	8.40	16.80	25.20	33.60	42.00	50.40	58.80	67.20	75.60	84.00
25 RUPEES	1977	28.50	500	14.30	0.46	.46	.92	1.84	2.76	3.68	4.60	9.20	13.80	18.40	23.00	27.60	32.20	36.80	41.40	46.00

Coin Denomination	Years of Issue	Coin Wt. Grams	Purity	Silver Wt. Grams	Silver Troy Oz.	Silver Value—U.S. Dollars														
						$1	$2	$4	$6	$8	$10	$20	$30	$40	$50	$60	$70	$80	$90	$100
SEYCHELLES - CONT'D.																				
25 RUPEES	1977	28.50	925	26.40	0.85	.85	1.70	3.40	5.10	6.80	8.50	17.00	25.50	34.00	42.50	51.00	59.50	68.00	76.50	85.00
50 RUPEES	1978	28.30	925	26.20	0.84	.84	1.68	3.36	5.04	6.72	8.40	16.80	25.20	33.60	42.00	50.40	58.80	67.20	75.60	84.00
100 RUPEES	1978	35.00	925	32.40	1.04	1.04	2.08	4.16	6.24	8.32	10.40	20.80	31.20	41.60	52.00	62.40	72.80	83.20	93.60	104.00
SHARJAH																				
5 RUPEES	1964	25.00	720	18.00	0.58	.58	1.16	2.32	3.48	4.64	5.80	11.60	17.40	23.20	29.00	34.80	40.60	46.40	52.20	58.00
1 RIYAL	1970	3.00	999	3.00	0.10	.10	.20	.40	.60	.80	1.00	2.00	3.00	4.00	5.00	6.00	7.00	8.00	9.00	10.00
2 RIYALS	1970	6.00	999	6.00	0.19	.19	.38	.76	1.14	1.52	1.90	3.80	5.70	7.60	9.50	11.40	13.30	15.20	17.10	19.00
5 RIYALS	1970	15.00	999	15.00	0.48	.48	.96	1.92	2.88	3.84	4.80	9.60	14.40	19.20	24.00	28.80	33.60	38.40	43.20	48.00
10 RIYALS	1970	30.00	999	30.00	0.96	.96	1.92	3.84	5.76	7.68	9.60	19.20	28.80	38.40	48.00	57.60	67.20	76.80	86.40	96.00
SIERRA LEONE																				
1 LEONE	1974	31.00	500	15.50	0.50	.50	1.00	2.00	3.00	4.00	5.00	10.00	15.00	20.00	25.00	30.00	35.00	40.00	45.00	50.00
1 LEONE	1964,1974	31.00	925	28.70	0.92	.92	1.84	3.68	5.52	7.36	9.20	18.40	27.60	36.80	46.00	55.20	64.40	73.60	82.80	92.00
SINGAPORE																				
1 DOLLAR	1975-1979	18.10	925	16.70	0.54	.54	1.08	2.16	3.24	4.32	5.40	10.80	16.20	21.60	27.00	32.40	37.80	43.20	48.60	54.00
5 DOLLARS	1973	25.00	500	12.50	0.40	.40	.80	1.60	2.40	3.20	4.00	8.00	12.00	16.00	20.00	24.00	28.00	32.00	36.00	40.00
10 DOLLARS	1972-1974	30.50	900	27.40	0.88	.88	1.76	3.52	5.28	7.04	8.80	17.60	26.40	35.20	44.00	52.80	61.60	70.40	79.20	88.00
10 DOLLARS	1975-1979	30.50	500	15.20	0.49	.49	.98	1.96	2.94	3.92	4.90	9.80	14.70	19.60	24.50	29.40	34.30	39.20	44.10	49.00
SOLOMON ISLANDS																				
5 DOLLARS	1977-1978	28.30	925	26.20	0.84	.84	1.68	3.36	5.04	6.72	8.40	16.80	25.20	33.60	42.00	50.40	58.80	67.20	75.60	84.00
5 DOLLARS	1978	27.30	925	25.20	0.81	.81	1.62	3.24	4.86	6.48	8.10	16.20	24.30	32.40	40.50	48.60	56.70	64.80	72.90	81.00
10 DOLLARS	1979	40.50	925	37.50	1.21	1.21	2.42	4.84	7.26	9.68	12.10	24.20	36.30	48.40	60.50	72.60	84.70	96.80	108.90	121.00
SOMALIA																				
50 CENTESIMI	1950	3.80	250	1.00	0.03	.03	.06	.12	.18	.24	.30	.60	.90	1.20	1.50	1.80	2.10	2.40	2.70	3.00
1 SOMALO	1950	7.60	250	1.90	0.06	.06	.12	.24	.36	.48	.60	1.20	1.80	2.40	3.00	3.60	4.20	4.80	5.40	6.00

Coin Denomination	Years of Issue	Coin Wt. Grams	Purity	Silver Wt. Grams	Silver Troy Oz.	Silver Value—U.S. Dollars														
						$1	$2	$4	$6	$8	$10	$20	$30	$40	$50	$60	$70	$80	$90	$100
SOUTH AFRICA {UNION OF}																				
3 PENCE	1923-1952	1.40	800	1.10	0.04	.04	.08	.16	.24	.32	.40	.80	1.20	1.60	2.00	2.40	2.80	3.20	3.60	4.00
3 PENCE	1953-1960	1.40	500	0.70	0.02	.02	.04	.08	.12	.16	.20	.40	.60	.80	1.00	1.20	1.40	1.60	1.80	2.00
6 PENCE	1923-1950	2.80	800	2.30	0.07	.07	.14	.28	.42	.56	.70	1.40	2.10	2.80	3.50	4.20	4.90	5.60	6.30	7.00
6 PENCE	1951-1960	2.80	500	1.40	0.05	.05	.10	.20	.30	.40	.50	1.00	1.50	2.00	2.50	3.00	3.50	4.00	4.50	5.00
1 SHILLING	1923-1950	5.70	800	4.50	0.14	.14	.28	.56	.84	1.12	1.40	2.80	4.20	5.60	7.00	8.40	9.80	11.20	12.60	14.00
1 SHILLING	1951-1960	5.70	500	2.80	0.09	.09	.18	.36	.54	.72	.90	1.80	2.70	3.60	4.50	5.40	6.30	7.20	8.10	9.00
1 FLORIN	1923-1930	11.30	800	9.00	0.29	.29	.58	1.16	1.74	2.32	2.90	5.80	8.70	11.60	14.50	17.40	18.90	23.20	26.10	29.00
2 SHILLINGS	1931-1950	11.30	800	9.00	0.29	.29	.58	1.16	1.74	2.32	2.90	5.80	8.70	11.60	14.50	17.40	18.90	23.20	26.10	29.00
2 SHILLINGS	1951-1960	11.30	500	5.70	0.18	.18	.36	.72	1.08	1.44	1.80	3.60	5.40	7.20	9.00	10.80	12.60	14.40	16.20	18.00
2-1/2 "	1923-1950	14.10	800	11.30	0.36	.36	.72	1.44	2.16	2.88	3.60	7.20	10.80	14.40	18.00	21.60	25.20	28.80	32.40	36.00
2-1/2 "	1951-1960	14.10	500	7.10	0.23	.23	.46	.92	1.38	1.84	2.30	4.60	6.90	9.20	11.50	13.80	16.10	18.40	20.70	23.00
5 SHILLING	1947-1950	28.30	800	22.60	0.73	.73	1.46	2.92	4.38	5.84	7.30	14.60	21.90	29.20	36.50	43.80	51.10	58.40	65.70	73.00
5 SHILLINGS	1951-1960	28.30	500	14.10	0.45	.45	.90	1.80	2.70	3.60	4.50	9.00	13.50	18.00	22.50	27.00	31.50	36.00	40.50	45.00
SOUTH AFRICA {REPUBLIC OF}																				
2-1/2 CENTS	1961-1964	1.40	500	0.70	0.02	.02	.04	.08	.12	.16	.20	.40	.60	.80	1.00	1.20	1.40	1.60	1.80	2.00
5 CENTS	1961-1964	2.80	500	1.40	0.05	.05	.10	.20	.30	.40	.50	1.00	1.50	2.00	2.50	3.00	3.50	4.00	4.50	5.00
10 CENTS	1961-1964	5.70	500	2.80	0.09	.09	.18	.36	.54	.72	.90	1.80	2.70	3.60	4.50	5.40	6.30	7.20	8.10	9.00
20 CENTS	1961-1964	11.30	500	5.70	0.18	.18	.36	.72	1.08	1.44	1.80	3.60	5.40	7.20	9.00	10.80	12.60	14.40	16.20	18.00
50 CENTS	1961-1964	28.30	500	14.10	0.45	.45	.90	1.80	2.70	3.60	4.50	9.00	13.50	18.00	22.50	27.00	31.50	36.00	40.50	45.00
1 RAND	1965-1978	15.00	800	12.00	0.39	.39	.78	1.56	2.34	3.12	3.90	7.80	11.70	15.60	19.50	23.40	27.30	31.20	35.10	39.00
SOUTHERN RHODESIA																				
1 CROWN	1953	29.10	500	14.50	0.47	.47	.94	1.88	2.82	3.76	4.70	9.40	14.10	18.80	23.50	28.20	32.90	37.60	42.30	47.00
SPAIN																				
5 CENTIMOS	1869-1926	2.50	835	2.10	0.07	.07	.14	.28	.42	.56	.70	1.40	2.10	2.80	3.50	4.20	4.90	5.60	6.30	7.00
1 PESETA	1869-1933	5.00	835	4.20	0.14	.14	.28	.56	.84	1.12	1.40	2.80	4.20	5.60	7.00	8.40	9.80	11.20	12.60	14.00
2 PESETAS	1869-1905	10.00	835	8.40	0.27	.27	.54	1.08	1.62	2.16	2.70	5.40	8.10	10.80	13.50	16.20	18.90	21.60	24.30	27.00
5 PESETAS	1869-1899	25.00	900	22.50	0.72	.72	1.44	2.88	4.32	5.76	7.20	14.40	21.60	28.80	36.00	43.20	50.40	57.60	64.80	72.00
100 PESETAS	1966	19.00	800	15.20	0.49	.49	.98	1.96	2.94	3.92	4.90	9.80	14.70	19.60	24.50	29.40	34.30	39.20	44.10	49.00
SUDAN																				
2-1/2 POUNDS	1976	20.30	925	26.20	0.84	.84	1.68	3.36	5.04	6.72	8.40	16.80	25.20	33.60	42.00	50.40	58.80	67.20	75.60	84.00
5 POUNDS	1976	35.00	925	32.40	1.04	1.04	2.08	4.16	6.24	8.32	10.40	20.80	31.20	41.60	52.00	62.40	72.80	83.20	93.60	104.00

Coin Denomination	Years of Issue	Coin Wt. Grams	Purity	Silver Wt. Grams	Silver Troy Oz.	Silver Value—U.S. Dollars $1	$2	$4	$6	$8	$10	$20	$30	$40	$50	$60	$70	$80	$90	$100
SUDAN - CONT'D.																				
5 POUNDS	1978	17.50	925	16.20	0.52	.52	1.04	2.08	3.12	4.16	5.20	10.40	15.60	20.80	26.00	31.20	36.40	41.60	46.80	52.00
10 POUNDS	1978	35.00	925	32.40	1.04	1.04	2.08	4.16	6.24	8.32	10.40	20.80	31.20	41.60	52.00	62.40	72.80	83.20	93.60	104.00
SURINAM																				
1 GULDEN	1962-1966	10.00	720	7.20	0.23	.23	.46	.92	1.38	1.84	2.30	4.60	6.90	9.20	11.50	13.80	16.10	18.40	20.70	23.00
SWAZILAND																				
5 CENTS	1967	2.50	800	2.00	0.06	.06	.12	.24	.36	.48	.60	1.20	1.80	2.40	3.00	3.60	4.20	4.80	5.40	6.00
10 CENTS	1968	4.00	800	3.20	0.10	.10	.20	.40	.60	.80	1.00	2.00	3.00	4.00	5.00	6.00	7.00	8.00	9.00	10.00
20 CENTS	1968	6.00	800	4.80	0.15	.15	.30	.60	.90	1.20	1.50	3.00	4.50	6.00	7.50	9.00	10.50	12.00	13.50	15.00
50 CENTS	1968	9.50	800	7.60	0.24	.24	.48	.96	1.44	1.92	2.40	4.80	7.20	9.60	12.00	14.40	16.80	19.20	21.60	24.00
1 LUHLANGA	1968	15.00	800	12.00	0.39	.39	.78	1.56	2.34	3.12	3.90	7.80	11.70	15.60	19.50	23.40	27.50	31.20	35.10	39.00
5 EMALANGENI	1974	10.30	925	9.50	0.31	.31	.62	1.24	1.86	2.48	3.10	6.20	9.30	12.40	15.50	18.60	21.70	24.80	27.90	31.00
7-1/2 "	1974	16.20	925	15.00	0.48	.48	.96	1.92	2.88	3.84	4.80	9.60	14.40	19.20	24.00	28.80	33.60	38.40	43.20	48.00
10 "	1975	25.50	925	23.60	0.76	.76	1.52	3.04	4.56	6.08	7.60	15.20	22.80	30.40	38.00	45.60	53.20	60.80	68.40	76.00
15 "	1974	32.60	925	30.10	0.97	.97	1.94	3.88	5.82	7.76	9.70	19.40	29.10	38.80	48.50	58.20	67.90	77.60	87.30	94.00
SWEDEN																				
10 ORE	1874-1962	1.50	400	0.60	0.02	.02	.04	.08	.12	.16	.20	.40	.60	.80	1.00	1.20	1.40	1.60	1.80	2.00
25 ORE	1874-1941	2.40	600	1.50	0.05	.05	.10	.20	.30	.40	.50	1.00	1.50	2.00	2.50	3.00	3.50	4.00	4.50	5.00
25 ORE	1943-1961	2.40	400	1.00	0.03	.03	.06	.12	.18	.24	.30	.60	.90	1.20	1.50	1.80	2.10	2.40	2.70	3.00
50 ORE	1875-1939	5.00	600	3.00	0.10	.10	.20	.40	.60	.80	1.00	2.00	3.00	4.00	5.00	6.00	7.00	8.00	9.00	10.00
50 ORE	1943-1961	5.00	400	2.00	0.06	.06	.12	.24	.36	.48	.60	1.20	1.80	2.40	3.00	3.60	4.20	4.80	5.40	6.00
1 KRONA	1875-1942	7.50	800	6.00	0.19	.19	.38	.76	1.14	1.52	1.90	3.80	5.70	7.60	9.50	11.40	13.30	15.20	17.10	19.00
1 KRONA	1942-1968	7.50	400	3.00	0.10	.10	.20	.40	.60	.80	1.00	2.00	3.00	4.00	5.00	6.00	7.00	8.00	9.00	10.00
2 KRONER	1876-1940	15.00	800	12.00	0.39	.39	.78	1.56	2.34	3.12	3.90	7.80	11.70	15.60	19.50	23.40	27.30	31.20	35.10	39.00
2 KRONER	1942-1966	15.00	400	6.00	0.19	.19	.38	.76	1.14	1.52	1.90	3.80	5.70	7.60	9.50	11.40	13.30	15.20	17.10	19.00
2 KRONER	1935	25.00	900	22.50	0.72	.72	1.44	2.88	4.32	5.76	7.20	14.40	21.60	28.80	36.00	43.20	50.40	57.60	64.80	72.00
5 KRONER	1952-1966	18.00	400	7.20	0.23	.23	.46	.92	1.38	1.84	2.30	4.60	6.90	9.20	11.50	13.80	16.10	18.40	20.70	23.00
10 KRONER	1972	18.00	830	14.90	0.48	.48	.96	1.92	2.88	3.84	4.80	9.60	14.40	19.20	24.00	28.80	33.60	38.40	43.20	48.00
50 KRONER	1975-1976	27.00	925	25.00	0.80	.80	1.60	3.20	4.80	6.40	8.00	16.00	24.00	32.00	40.00	48.00	56.00	64.00	72.00	80.00
SWITZERLAND																				
1/2 FRANC	1875-1967	2.50	835	2.10	0.07	.07	.14	.28	.42	.56	.70	1.40	2.10	2.80	3.50	4.20	4.90	5.60	6.30	7.00

Coin Denomination	Years of Issue	Coin Wt. Grams	Purity	Silver Wt. Grams	Silver Troy Oz.	Silver Value—U.S. Dollars $1	$2	$4	$6	$8	$10	$20	$30	$40	$50	$60	$70	$80	$90	$100
SWITZERLAND - CONT'D.																				
1 FRANC	1875-1967	5.00	835	4.20	0.14	.14	.28	.56	.84	1.12	1.40	2.80	4.20	5.60	7.00	8.40	9.80	11.20	12.60	14.00
2 FRANCS	1874-1967	10.00	835	8.40	0.27	.27	.54	1.08	1.62	2.16	2.70	5.40	8.10	10.80	13.50	16.20	18.90	21.60	24.30	27.00
5 FRANCS	1931-1969	15.00	835	12.50	0.40	.40	.80	1.60	2.40	3.20	4.00	8.00	12.00	16.00	20.00	24.00	28.00	32.00	36.00	40.00
SYRIA																				
10 PIASTRES	1929	2.50	680	1.70	0.05	.05	.10	.20	.30	.40	.50	1.00	1.50	2.00	2.50	3.00	3.50	4.00	4.50	5.00
25 PIASTRES	1929-1937	5.00	680	3.40	0.11	.11	.22	.44	.66	.88	1.10	2.20	3.30	4.40	5.50	6.60	7.70	8.80	9.90	11.00
50 PIASTRES	1929-1937	10.00	680	6.80	0.22	.22	.44	.88	1.32	1.76	2.20	4.40	6.60	8.80	11.00	13.20	15.40	17.60	19.80	22.00
TANZANIA																				
25 SHILINGI	1974	25.30	500	12.70	0.41	.41	.82	1.64	2.46	3.28	4.10	8.20	12.30	16.40	20.50	24.60	28.70	32.80	36.90	41.00
25 SHILINGI	1974	28.30	925	26.20	0.84	.84	1.68	3.36	5.04	6.72	8.40	16.80	25.20	33.60	42.00	50.40	58.80	67.20	75.60	84.00
50 SHILINGI	1974	31.70	500	15.80	0.51	.51	1.02	2.04	3.06	4.08	5.10	10.20	15.30	20.40	25.50	30.60	35.70	40.80	45.90	51.00
50 SHILINGI	1974	35.00	925	32.40	1.04	1.04	2.08	4.16	6.24	8.32	10.40	20.80	31.20	41.60	52.00	62.40	72.80	83.20	93.60	104.00
THAILAND																				
20 BAHT	1963	20.00	750	15.00	0.48	.48	.96	1.92	2.88	3.84	4.80	9.60	14.40	19.20	24.00	28.80	33.60	38.40	43.20	48.00
50 BAHT	1970	25.00	900	22.50	0.72	.72	1.44	2.88	4.32	5.76	7.20	14.40	21.60	28.80	36.00	43.20	50.40	57.60	64.80	72.00
50 BAHT	1974	25.00	400	10.00	0.32	.32	.64	1.28	1.92	2.56	3.20	6.40	9.60	12.80	16.00	19.20	22.40	25.60	28.80	32.00
50 BAHT	1974	25.30	500	12.70	0.41	.41	.82	1.64	2.46	3.28	4.10	8.20	12.30	16.40	20.50	24.60	28.70	32.80	36.90	41.00
50 BAHT	1974	28.30	925	26.20	0.84	.84	1.68	3.36	5.04	6.72	8.40	16.80	25.20	33.60	42.00	50.40	58.80	67.20	75.60	84.00
100 BAHT	1974	31.70	500	15.80	0.51	.51	1.02	2.04	3.06	4.08	5.10	10.20	15.30	20.40	25.50	30.60	35.70	40.80	45.90	51.00
100 BAHT	1975	25.00	500	12.50	0.40	.40	.80	1.60	2.40	3.20	4.00	8.00	12.00	16.00	20.00	24.00	28.00	32.00	36.00	40.00
150 BAHT	1975-1978	22.00	925	20.40	0.66	.66	1.32	2.64	3.96	5.28	6.60	13.20	19.80	26.40	33.00	39.60	46.20	52.80	59.40	66.00
200 BAHT	1979	22.10	500	11.10	0.36	.36	.72	1.44	2.16	2.88	3.60	7.20	10.80	14.40	18.00	21.60	25.50	28.80	32.40	36.00
TONGA																				
5 PAANGA	1975	31.00	999	31.00	1.00	1.00	2.00	4.00	6.00	8.00	10.00	20.00	30.00	40.00	50.00	60.00	70.00	80.00	90.00	100.00
10 PAANGA	1975	62.00	999	62.00	2.00	2.00	4.00	8.00	12.00	16.00	20.00	40.00	60.00	80.00	100.00	120.00	140.00	160.00	180.00	200.00
20 PAANGA	1975	140.00	999	140.00	4.50	4.50	9.00	18.00	27.00	36.00	45.00	90.00	135.00	180.00	225.00	270.00	315.00	360.00	405.00	450.00

Coin Denomination	Years of Issue	Coin Wt. Grams	Purity	Silver Wt. Grams	Silver Troy Oz.	Silver Value—U.S. Dollars $1	$2	$4	$6	$8	$10	$20	$30	$40	$50	$60	$70	$80	$90	$100
TRINIDAD - TOBAGO																				
5 DOLLARS	1971-1979	29.70	925	27.50	0.88	.88	1.76	3.52	5.28	7.04	8.80	17.60	26.40	35.20	44.00	52.80	61.60	70.40	79.20	88.00
10 DOLLARS	1972-1979	35.00	925	32.40	1.04	1.04	2.08	4.16	6.24	8.32	10.40	20.80	31.20	41.60	52.00	62.40	72.80	83.20	93.60	104.00
TRISTAN DA CUNHA																				
25 PENCE	1977	28.30	925	26.20	0.84	.84	1.68	3.36	5.04	6.72	8.40	16.80	25.20	33.60	42.00	50.40	58.80	67.20	75.60	84.00
1 CROWN	1978	28.80	925	26.20	0.84	.84	1.68	3.36	5.04	6.72	8.40	16.80	25.20	33.60	42.00	50.40	58.80	67.20	75.60	84.00
TUNISIA																				
50 CENTIMES	1891-1918	2.50	835	2.10	0.07	.07	.14	.28	.42	.56	.70	1.40	2.10	2.80	3.50	4.20	4.90	5.60	6.30	7.00
1 FRANC	1891-1928	5.00	835	4.20	0.14	.14	.28	.56	.84	1.12	1.40	2.80	4.20	5.60	7.00	8.40	9.80	11.20	12.60	14.00
2 FRANCS	1891-1928	10.80	835	8.40	0.27	.27	.54	1.08	1.62	2.16	2.70	5.40	8.10	10.80	13.50	16.20	18.90	21.60	24.30	27.00
5 FRANCS	1934-1939	5.00	680	3.40	0.11	.11	.22	.44	.66	.88	1.10	2.20	3.30	4.40	5.50	6.60	7.70	8.80	9.90	11.00
10 FRANCS	1930-1939	10.00	680	6.80	0.22	.22	.44	.88	1.32	1.76	2.20	4.40	6.60	8.80	11.00	13.20	15.40	17.60	19.80	22.00
20 FRANCS	1930-1939	20.00	680	13.60	0.44	.44	.88	1.76	2.64	3.52	4.40	8.80	13.20	17.60	22.00	26.40	30.80	35.20	39.60	44.00
1 DINAR	1969	20.00	925	18.50	0.59	.59	1.18	2.36	3.54	4.72	5.90	11.80	17.70	23.60	29.50	35.40	41.30	47.20	53.10	59.00
1 DINAR	1970	18.00	680	12.20	0.39	.39	.78	1.56	2.34	3.12	3.90	7.80	11.70	15.60	19.50	23.40	27.30	31.20	35.10	39.00
TURKEY																				
1 PIASTRE	1277-1327	1.20	830	1.00	0.03	.03	.06	.12	.18	.24	.30	.60	.90	1.20	1.50	1.80	2.10	2.40	2.70	3.00
2 PIASTRES	1255-1327	2.40	830	2.00	0.06	.06	.12	.24	.36	.48	.60	1.20	1.80	2.40	3.00	3.60	4.20	4.80	5.40	6.00
5 PIASTRES	1255-1327	6.00	830	5.00	0.16	.16	.32	.64	.96	1.28	1.60	3.20	4.80	6.40	8.00	9.60	11.20	12.80	14.40	16.00
10 PIASTRES	1255-1327	12.00	830	10.00	0.32	.32	.64	1.28	1.92	2.56	3.20	6.40	9.60	12.80	16.00	19.20	22.40	25.60	28.80	34.00
20 PIASTRES	1255-1327	24.10	830	20.00	0.64	.64	1.28	2.56	3.84	5.12	6.40	12.80	19.20	25.60	32.00	38.40	44.80	51.20	57.60	64.00
25 KURUS	1935-1937	3.00	830	2.50	0.08	.08	.16	.32	.48	.64	.80	1.60	2.40	3.20	4.00	4.80	5.60	6.40	7.20	8.00
50 KURUS	1935-1937	6.00	830	5.00	0.16	.16	.32	.64	.96	1.28	1.60	3.20	4.80	6.40	8.00	9.60	11.20	12.80	14.40	16.00
50 KURUS	1947-1948	3.50	600	2.00	0.07	.07	.14	.28	.42	.56	.70	1.40	2.10	2.80	3.50	4.20	4.90	5.60	6.30	7.00
100 KURUS	1934-1939	12.00	830	10.00	0.32	.32	.64	1.28	1.92	2.56	3.20	6.40	9.60	12.80	16.00	19.20	22.40	25.60	28.80	32.00
1 LIRA	1937-1941	12.00	830	10.00	0.32	.32	.64	1.28	1.92	2.56	3.20	6.40	9.60	12.80	16.00	19.20	22.40	25.60	28.80	32.00
1 LIRA	1947-1948	7.50	600	4.50	0.14	.14	.28	.56	.84	1.12	1.40	2.80	4.20	5.60	7.00	8.40	9.80	11.20	12.60	14.00
10 LIRA	1960	15.00	830	12.50	0.40	.40	.80	1.60	2.40	3.20	4.00	8.00	12.00	16.00	20.00	24.00	28.00	32.00	36.00	40.00
25 LIRA	1970	15.00	830	0.50	0.02	.02	.04	.08	.12	.16	.20	.40	.60	.80	1.00	1.20	1.40	1.60	1.80	2.00
50 LIRA	1971-1972	19.00	830	15.80	0.51	.51	1.02	2.04	3.06	4.08	5.10	10.20	15.30	20.40	25.50	30.60	35.70	40.80	49.50	51.00
50 LIRA	1973-1977	13.00	900	11.70	0.38	.38	.76	1.52	2.28	3.04	3.80	7.60	11.40	15.20	19.00	22.80	26.60	30.40	34.20	38.00
100 LIRA	1973	22.00	900	19.80	0.64	.64	1.28	2.56	3.84	5.12	6.40	12.80	19.20	25.60	32.00	38.40	44.80	51.20	57.60	64.00
150 LIRA	1978	8.90	800	7.10	0.23	.23	.46	.92	1.38	1.84	2.30	4.60	6.90	9.20	11.50	13.80	16.10	18.40	20.70	23.00
200 LIRA	1978	9.00	830	7.50	0.24	.24	.48	.96	1.44	1.92	2.40	4.80	7.20	9.60	12.00	14.40	16.80	19.20	21.60	24.00
ABOVE DATES INCLUDE AH DATES.																				

Coin Denomination	Years of Issue	Coin Wt. Grams	Purity	Silver Wt. Grams	Silver Troy Oz.	Silver Value—U.S. Dollars														
						$1	$2	$4	$6	$8	$10	$20	$30	$40	$50	$60	$70	$80	$90	$100
TURKS AND CAICOS ISLANDS																				
5 CROWNS	1975-1976	20.30	500	12.20	0.39	.39	.78	1.56	2.34	3.12	3.90	7.80	11.70	15.60	19.50	23.40	27.30	31.20	36.10	38.00
10 CROWNS	1975-1976, 1979	29.80	925	27.60	0.89	.89	1.78	3.56	5.34	7.12	8.90	17.80	26.70	35.60	44.50	53.40	62.30	71.20	80.10	89.00
20 CROWNS	1974-1978	28.80	925	35.90	1.15	1.15	2.30	4.60	6.90	9.20	11.50	23.00	34.50	46.00	57.50	69.00	80.50	92.00	103.50	115.00
25 CROWNS	1977-1978	43.70	925	40.50	1.30	1.30	2.60	5.20	7.80	10.40	13.00	26.00	39.00	52.00	65.00	78.00	91.00	104.00	117.00	132.00
TUVALU																				
5 DOLLARS	1976	28.30	925	26.20	0.84	.84	1.68	3.36	5.04	6.72	8.40	16.80	25.20	33.60	42.00	50.40	58.80	67.20	75.60	84.00
UGANDA																				
2 SCHILLINGS	1969-1970	4.00	1000	4.00	0.13	.13	.26	.52	.78	1.04	1.30	2.60	3.90	5.20	6.50	7.80	9.10	10.40	11.70	13.00
5 SCHILLINGS	1969-1970	10.00	1000	10.00	0.32	.32	.64	1.28	1.92	2.56	3.20	6.40	9.60	12.80	16.00	19.20	22.40	25.60	28.80	32.00
10 SCHILLINGS	1969-1970	20.00	1000	20.00	0.64	.64	1.28	2.56	3.84	5.12	6.40	12.80	19.20	25.60	32.00	38.40	44.80	51.20	57.60	64.00
20 SCHILLINGS	1969-1970	40.00	1000	40.00	1.29	1.29	2.58	5.16	7.74	10.32	12.90	25.80	38.70	51.60	64.50	77.40	90.30	103.00	116.10	129.00
25 SCHILLINGS	1969-1970	50.00	1000	50.00	1.61	1.61	3.22	6.44	9.66	12.88	16.10	32.20	48.30	64.40	80.50	96.60	112.70	128.80	144.90	161.00
30 SCHILLINGS	1969-1970	60.00	1000	60.00	1.93	1.93	3.86	7.72	11.58	15.44	19.30	38.60	57.90	77.20	96.50	115.80	135.10	154.40	173.70	193.00
UMMAL - QUIWAIN																				
1 RIYAL	1970	3.00	999	3.00	0.10	.10	.20	.40	.60	.80	1.00	2.00	3.00	4.00	5.00	6.00	7.00	8.00	9.00	10.00
2 RIYALS	1970	6.00	999	6.00	0.19	.19	.38	.76	1.14	1.52	1.90	3.80	5.70	7.60	9.50	11.40	13.30	15.20	17.10	19.00
5 RIYALS	1970	15.00	999	15.00	0.48	.48	.96	1.92	2.88	3.84	4.80	9.60	14.40	19.20	24.00	28.80	33.60	38.40	43.20	48.00
10 RIYALS	1970	30.00	999	30.00	0.96	.96	1.92	3.84	5.76	7.68	9.60	19.20	28.80	38.40	48.00	57.60	67.20	76.80	86.40	96.00
UNITED STATES OF AMERICA																				
10 CENTS	1837-1964	2.50	900	2.30	0.07	.07	.14	.28	.42	.56	.70	1.40	2.10	2.80	3.50	4.20	4.90	5.60	6.30	7.00
25 CENTS	1838-1964	6.30	900	5.60	0.18	.18	.36	.72	1.08	1.44	1.80	3.60	5.40	7.20	9.00	10.80	12.60	14.40	16.20	18.00
50 CENTS	1839-1964	12.50	900	11.30	0.36	.36	.72	1.44	2.16	2.88	3.60	7.20	10.80	14.40	18.00	21.60	25.50	28.80	32.40	36.00
1 DOLLAR	1878-1935	26.70	900	24.10	0.77	.77	1.54	3.08	4.62	6.16	7.70	15.40	23.10	30.80	38.50	46.20	53.90	61.60	69.30	77.00
50 CENTS	1965-1970	11.50	400	4.60	0.15	.15	.30	.60	.90	1.20	1.50	3.00	4.50	6.00	7.50	9.00	10.50	12.00	13.50	15.00
1 DOLLAR	1971-1978	24.50	400	9.90	0.32	.32	.64	1.28	1.92	2.56	3.20	6.40	9.60	12.80	16.00	19.20	22.40	25.60	28.80	32.00

Coin Denomination	Years of Issue	Coin Wt. Grams	Purity	Silver Wt. Grams	Silver Troy Oz.	Silver Value—U.S. Dollars														
						$1	$2	$4	$6	$8	$10	$20	$30	$40	$50	$60	$70	$80	$90	$100
URUGUAY																				
10 CENTIMAS	1877-1893	2.50	900	2.30	0.07	.07	.14	.28	.42	.56	.60	1.20	2.10	2.80	3.50	4.20	4.90	5.60	6.30	7.00
20 CENTIMAS	1877-1893	5.00	900	4.50	0.14	.14	.28	.56	.84	1.12	1.40	2.80	4.20	5.60	7.00	8.40	9.80	11.20	12.60	14.00
20 CENTIMAS	1920-1930	5.00	800	4.00	0.13	.13	.26	.52	.78	1.04	1.30	2.60	3.90	5.20	6.50	7.80	9.10	10.40	11.70	13.00
20 CENTIMAS	1942,1954	3.00	720	2.20	0.07	.07	.14	.28	.42	.56	.70	1.40	2.10	2.80	3.50	4.20	4.90	5.60	6.30	7.00
50 CENTIMAS	1877-1894	12.50	900	11.30	0.36	.36	.72	1.44	2.16	2.88	3.60	7.20	10.80	14.40	18.00	21.60	25.50	28.80	32.40	36.00
50 CENTIMAS	1916-1917	12.50	900	11.30	0.36	.36	.72	1.44	2.16	2.88	3.60	7.20	10.80	14.40	18.00	21.60	25.50	28.80	32.40	36.00
50 CENTIMAS	1943	4.50	720	3.20	0.10	.10	.20	.40	.60	.80	1.00	2.00	3.00	4.00	5.00	6.00	7.00	8.00	9.00	10.00
1 PESO	1877-1917	25.00	900	22.50	0.72	.72	1.44	2.88	4.32	5.76	7.20	14.40	21.60	28.80	36.00	43.20	50.40	57.60	64.80	72.00
1 PESO	1942	9.00	720	6.50	0.21	.21	.42	.84	1.26	1.68	2.10	4.20	6.30	8.40	10.50	12.60	14.70	16.80	18.90	21.00
10 PESOS	1961	12.50	900	11.30	0.36	.36	.72	1.44	2.16	2.88	3.60	7.20	10.80	14.40	18.00	21.60	25.50	28.80	32.40	36.00
1000 PESOS	1969	25.00	900	22.50	0.72	.72	1.44	2.88	4.32	5.76	7.20	14.40	21.60	28.80	36.00	43.20	50.40	57.60	64.80	72.00
VATICAN CITY																				
5 LIRE	1929-1946	5.00	835	4.20	0.14	.14	.28	.56	.84	1.12	1.40	2.80	4.20	5.60	7.00	8.40	9.80	11.20	12.60	14.00
10 LIRE	1929-1946	10.00	835	8.40	0.27	.27	.54	1.08	1.62	2.16	2.70	5.40	8.10	10.80	13.50	16.20	18.90	21.60	24.30	27.00
500 LIRE	1958-1978	11.00	835	9.20	0.30	.30	.60	1.20	1.80	2.40	3.00	6.00	9.00	12.00	15.00	18.00	21.00	24.00	27.00	30.00
VENEZUELA																				
25 CENTIMOS	1954-1960	1.30	835	1.00	0.03	.03	.06	.12	.18	.24	.30	.60	.90	1.20	1.50	1.80	2.10	2.40	2.70	3.00
50 CENTIMOS	1954-1960	2.50	835	2.10	0.07	.07	.14	.28	.42	.56	.70	1.40	2.10	2.80	3.50	4.20	4.90	5.60	6.30	7.00
1/4 BOLIVAR	1894-1948	1.30	835	1.00	0.03	.03	.06	.12	.18	.24	.30	.60	.90	1.20	1.50	1.80	2.10	2.40	2.70	3.00
1/2 BOLIVAR	1879-1946	2.50	835	2.10	0.07	.07	.14	.28	.42	.56	.70	1.40	2.10	2.80	3.50	4.20	4.90	5.60	6.30	7.00
1 BOLIVAR	1879-1965	5.00	835	4.20	0.14	.14	.28	.56	.84	1.12	1.40	2.80	4.20	5.60	7.00	8.40	9.80	11.20	12.60	14.00
2 BOLIVARS	1879-1965	10.00	835	8.40	0.27	.27	.54	1.08	1.62	2.16	2.70	5.40	8.10	10.80	13.50	16.20	18.90	21.60	24.30	27.00
5 BOLIVARS	1879-1936	25.00	900	22.50	0.72	.72	1.44	2.88	4.32	5.76	7.20	14.40	21.60	28.80	36.00	43.20	50.40	57.60	64.80	72.00
10 BOLIVARS	1973	30.00	900	27.00	0.87	.87	1.74	3.48	5.22	6.96	8.70	17.40	26.10	34.80	43.50	52.20	60.90	69.60	78.30	87.00
25 BOLIVARS	1975	28.30	925	26.20	0.84	.84	1.68	3.36	5.04	6.72	8.40	16.80	25.20	33.60	42.00	50.40	58.80	67.20	75.60	84.00
50 BOLIVARS	1975	35.00	925	32.40	1.04	1.04	2.08	4.16	6.24	8.32	10.40	20.80	31.20	41.60	52.00	62.40	72.80	83.20	93.60	104.00
WEST AFRICAN STATES																				
500 FRANCS	1972	25.00	900	22.50	0.72	.72	1.44	2.88	4.32	5.76	7.20	14.40	21.60	28.80	36.00	43.20	50.40	57.60	64.80	72.00

Coin Denomination	Years of Issue	Coin Wt. Grams	Purity	Silver Wt. Grams	Silver Troy Oz.	Silver Value—U.S. Dollars $1	$2	$4	$6	$8	$10	$20	$30	$40	$50	$60	$70	$80	$90	$100
WESTERN SAMOA																				
1 SENE	1974	0.30	925	0.03	0.01	.01	.02	.04	.06	.08	.10	.20	.30	.40	.50	.60	.70	.80	.90	1.00
2 SENE	1974	0.50	925	0.05	0.02	.02	.04	.08	.12	.16	.20	.40	.60	.80	1.00	1.20	1.40	1.60	1.80	2.00
5 SENE	1974	1.40	925	1.30	0.04	.04	.08	.16	.24	.32	.40	.80	1.20	1.60	2.00	2.40	2.80	3.20	3.60	4.00
10 SENE	1974	2.70	925	2.50	0.08	.08	.16	.32	.48	.64	.80	1.60	2.40	3.20	4.00	4.80	5.60	6.40	7.20	8.00
20 SENE	1974	5.50	925	5.10	0.16	.16	.32	.64	.96	1.28	1.60	3.20	4.80	6.40	8.00	9.60	11.20	12.80	14.40	16.00
50 SENE	1974	13.70	925	12.70	0.41	.41	.82	1.64	2.46	3.28	4.10	8.20	12.30	16.40	20.50	24.60	28.70	32.80	36.90	41.00
1 TALA	1967-1978	27.30	925	25.20	0.81	.81	1.62	3.24	4.86	6.48	8.10	16.20	24.30	32.40	40.50	48.60	56.70	64.80	72.90	81.00
1 TALA	1979	27.30	500	13.60	0.44	.44	.88	1.76	2.64	3.52	4.40	8.80	13.20	17.60	22.00	26.40	30.80	35.20	39.60	44.00
YEMEN																				
1 RIAL	1965	24.90	720	17.90	0.58	.58	1.16	2.32	3.48	4.64	5.80	11.60	17.40	23.20	29.00	34.80	40.60	46.40	52.20	58.00
2 BUGSHA	1963	1.00	720	0.70	0.02	.02	.04	.08	.12	.16	.20	.40	.60	.80	1.00	1.20	1.40	1.60	1.80	2.00
4 BUGSHA	1963	2.00	720	1.40	0.05	.05	.10	.20	.30	.40	.50	1.00	1.50	2.00	2.50	3.00	3.50	4.00	4.50	5.00
5 BUGSHA	1963	2.50	720	1.80	0.06	.06	.12	.24	.36	.48	.60	1.20	1.80	2.40	3.00	3.60	4.20	4.80	5.40	6.00
8 BUGSHA	1963	4.00	720	2.90	0.09	.09	.18	.36	.54	.72	.90	1.80	2.70	3.60	4.50	5.40	6.30	7.20	8.10	9.00
10 BUGSHA	1963	5.00	720	3.60	0.12	.12	.24	.48	.72	.96	1.20	2.40	3.60	4.80	6.00	7.20	8.40	9.60	10.80	12.00
20 BUGSHA	1963	10.00	720	7.20	0.23	.23	.46	.92	1.38	1.84	2.30	4.60	6.90	9.20	11.50	13.80	16.10	18.40	20.70	23.00
1 RIAL	1963	20.00	720	14.40	0.46	.46	.92	1.84	2.76	3.68	4.60	9.20	13.80	18.40	23.00	27.60	32.20	36.80	41.40	46.00
1 RIYAL	1969	12.00	925	11.10	0.36	.36	.72	1.44	2.16	2.88	3.60	7.20	10.80	14.40	18.00	21.60	25.50	28.80	32.40	36.00
2 RIYALS	1969	25.00	925	23.10	0.74	.74	1.48	2.96	4.44	5.92	7.40	14.80	22.20	29.60	37.00	44.40	51.80	59.20	66.60	74.00
YUGOSLAVIA																				
10 DINARA	1931	7.00	500	3.50	0.11	.11	.22	.44	.66	.88	1.10	2.20	3.30	4.40	5.50	6.60	7.70	8.80	9.90	11.00
20 DINARA	1931	14.00	500	7.00	0.23	.23	.46	.92	1.38	1.84	2.30	4.60	6.90	9.20	11.50	13.80	16.10	18.40	20.70	23.00
20 DINARA	1938	9.00	750	6.80	0.22	.22	.44	.88	1.32	1.76	2.20	4.40	6.60	8.80	11.00	13.20	15.40	17.60	19.80	22.00
20 DINARA	1968	9.00	925	8.30	0.27	.27	.54	1.08	1.62	2.16	2.70	5.40	8.10	10.80	13.50	16.20	18.90	21.60	24.30	27.00
50 DINARA	1932	23.30	750	17.50	0.56	.56	1.12	2.24	3.36	4.48	5.60	11.20	16.80	22.40	28.00	33.60	39.20	44.80	50.40	56.00
50 DINARA	1938	15.00	750	11.30	0.36	.36	.72	1.44	2.16	2.88	3.60	7.20	10.80	14.40	18.00	21.60	25.50	28.80	32.40	36.00
50 DINARA	1968	10.00	925	18.50	0.59	.59	1.18	2.36	3.54	4.72	5.90	11.80	17.70	23.60	29.50	35.40	41.30	47.20	53.10	59.00
YUGOSLAVIA - SERBIA																				
50 PARE	1875-1915	2.50	835	2.10	0.07	.07	.14	.28	.42	.56	.70	1.40	2.10	2.80	3.50	4.20	4.70	5.60	6.30	7.00
1 DINAR	1875-1915	5.00	835	4.20	0.14	.14	.28	.56	.84	1.12	1.40	2.80	4.20	5.60	7.00	8.40	9.80	11.20	12.60	14.00
2 DINARA	1875-1915	10.00	835	8.40	0.27	.27	.54	1.08	1.62	2.16	2.70	5.40	8.10	10.80	13.50	16.20	18.90	21.60	24.30	27.00

Coin Denomination	Years of Issue	Coin Wt. Grams	Purity	Silver Wt. Grams	Silver Troy Oz.	Silver Value—U.S. Dollars														
						$1	$2	$4	$6	$8	$10	$20	$30	$40	$50	$60	$70	$80	$90	$100
ZAIRE																				
2 ZAIRES	1975	28.30	925	26.20	0.84	.84	1.68	3.36	5.04	6.72	8.40	16.80	25.20	33.60	42.00	50.40	58.80	67.20	75.60	84.00
5 ZAIRES	1975	35.00	925	32.40	1.04	1.04	2.08	4.16	6.24	8.32	10.40	20.80	31.20	41.60	52.00	62.40	72.80	83.20	93.60	104.00
ZAMBIA																				
5 KWACHA	1979	28.30	925	26.20	0.84	.84	1.68	3.36	5.04	6.72	8.40	16.80	25.20	33.60	42.00	50.40	58.80	67.20	75.60	84.00
10 KWACHA	1979	35.00	925	32.40	1.04	1.04	1.08	4.16	6.24	8.32	10.40	20.80	31.20	41.60	52.00	62.40	72.80	83.20	93.60	104.00

Notes

Notes

Notes

Notes

Notes

Notes

Notes

Notes

Notes

Notes